THE CHRISTIAN MOTHER GOOSE® BIG BOOK

Un Petit Enfant Les Conduira

Dedicated with love to my husband, Dale, and sons — Glen, Bradley, Kevin and Keith; the five men God gave me to enrich my life with adventure, serendipity and endearing love.

Copyright © 1992 Marjorie Decker

ISBN 0-529-07315-3
Library of Congress Catalog Card 92-60502

Printed in the United States of America.
First Printing, June 1992
Second Printing, March 1993

Published by
WORLD BIBLE PUBLISHERS, INC.
1500 Riverside Drive
Iowa Falls, Iowa 50126

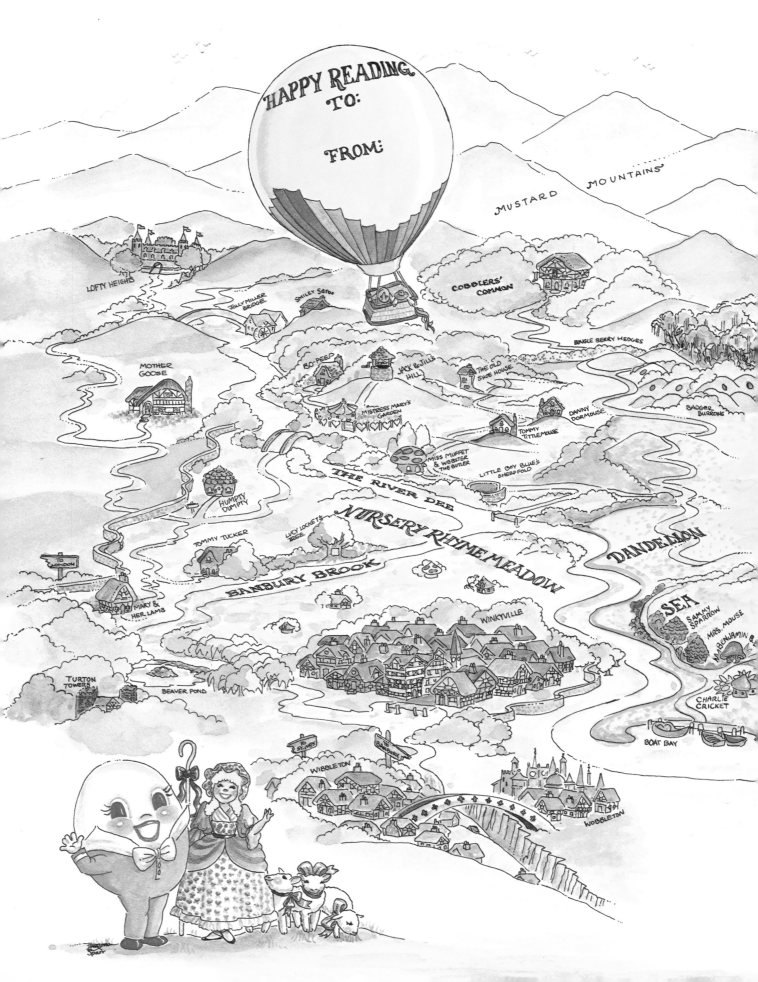

THE **CHRISTIAN MOTHER GOOSE**® **BIG BOOK**

written by
Marjorie Ainsborough Decker

Illustrated by
Theanna Sparr
Colleen Murphy Scott
Glenna Fae Hammond
Marjorie Ainsborough Decker

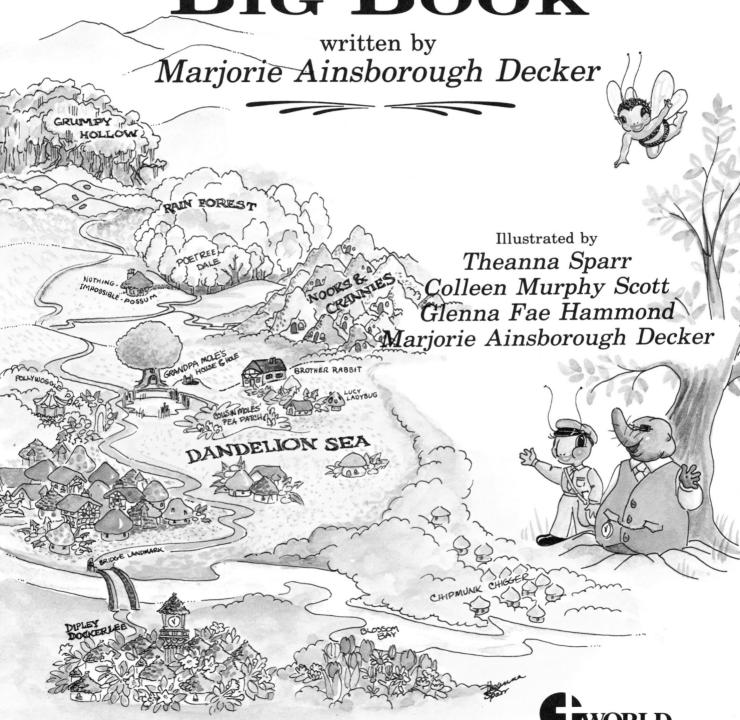

GRUMPY HOLLOW

RAIN FOREST

POETREE DALE

NOTHING-IMPOSSIBLE-POSSUM

NOOKS & CRANNIES

POLLYWOGGLE

GRANDPA MOLE'S HOUSE & HOLE

BROTHER RABBIT

LUCY LADYBUG

COUSIN MOLES' PEA PATCH

DANDELION SEA

BRIDGE LANDMARK

DIPLEY DOCKERLEE

BLOSSOM BAY

CHIPMUNK CHIGGER

WORLD
Bible Publishers, Inc.
Iowa Falls, Iowa

BIG BOOK CONTENTS

OFF TO THE FEAST OF REJOICING!

"Hurray! Hurray! It's a new today!
My balloon is up and we're hoisting;
There's much to be done,
So get up with the sun,
And prepare for the Feast of Rejoicing!"

Up, up and away, without delay,
And with Grandpa Mole cheery-voicing,
The balloon so grand,
Sailed over the land
To announce the Feast of Rejoicing!

6

"Friends, bring good fare, for all to share
In God's love and goodness, together.
It's a day to enjoy,
Old or young, girl or boy,
Celebrate in the finest of weather!"

Grandpa Mole's loud shout very soon brought out
Humpty Dumpty, and Miss Muffet, too.
And Little Bo-Peep,
With all her sheep,
Ran to tell her friend, Little Boy Blue.

Mother Goose from the air, dropped everywhere,
The announcements of time and of place.
On every hillside
Windows popped open wide,
"Yes, we're coming!" called each cheery face.

"Now that's very nice," said the Three Kind Mice,
"We'll take cheese and we'll start out quite soon.
At the top of the hill,
We'll remind Jack and Jill
To be at the park by twelve, noon."

8

With rustle and bustle, and tussle and hustle,
Frogs, chipmunks and crickets and beavers,
With otters and moles,
Are leaving house-holes,
For the Feast of Rejoicing believers!

So, come little guest to the Feast with the rest,
You'll hear stories you'll quite understand;
Now open the book,
And listen and look
At the life in this wonderful land.

MARY'S LAMB

Mary had a little lamb,
　Its fleece was white as snow,
And everywhere that Mary went
　The lamb was sure to go.

Now, Jesus has a little lamb,
　That little lamb is you!
And He is pleased
　When all His lambs
Keep following Him, too.

THERE WAS AN OLD WOMAN

There was an old woman
    Who lived in a shoe.
She had so many children,
    And loved them all, too.
She said, "Thank you, Lord Jesus,
    For sending them bread,"
Then kissed them all gladly
    And sent them to bed.

11

HUMPTY DUMPTY

Humpty Dumpty sat on a wall,
  Humpty Dumpty had a great fall;
Humpty Dumpty shouted, "Amen!
  God can put me together again."

IF I HAD A DONKEY

If I had a donkey
  That wouldn't go,
Would I beat him?
  Oh, no, no, no!
I'd stroke his little nose
  And give him some hay,
Then tell him I needed him
  To ride a mile away.

12

I SEE THE MOON

I see the moon,
   And the moon sees me.
God bless the moon,
   And God bless me!

THERE WAS A LITTLE GIRL

There was a little girl
   Who found a little pearl,
And then found ten more, twice!
   She sold them all to buy
What her little eye did spy...
   One BIG PEARL of great price!

THREE KIND MICE

Three kind mice,
　See what they've done!
They helped a lost chick
　To find Mother Hen,
They brought some food
　To the church mice, then
They cleaned up the tree house
　For Jenny Wren,
Those three kind mice.

LITTLE LUCY LADYBUG

Little Lucy Ladybug
   How do you take a bath?

Oh, I have a lovely bathtub
   Beside my garden path.
It is a yellow buttercup,
   And when it fills with rain,
I jump into my yellow bath
   And jump out clean again.

Little Lucy Ladybug
   Where do you go to bed?

Oh, I have a lovely bedroom
   Where I lay my little head.
It is a pretty daisy,
   And its sheets are sparkling white.
My pillow is a golden puff
   I sleep on through the night.

Little Lucy Ladybug
   Who cares for you each day?

Oh, I have a lovely Someone,
   And I'll tell you, if I may…
He is the Heavenly Father,
   Who made my bath—and bedroom, too;
And kindly watches over me,
   And cares for me…and you!

TWINKLE, TWINKLE

Twinkle, twinkle, little star,
  God has placed you where you are;
Up above the world so high,
  You're God's light hung in the sky.

Twinkle, twinkle, little star,
  When you look down from afar,
What's the little light you see
  Shining here for God? It's me!

Twinkle, twinkle, little star,
  I can't reach you in a car;
But someday, by Jesus' might,
  I'll fly to visit you each night.

Twinkle, twinkle, little star,
  God has placed you where you are!

JUMPING JOAN

Here am I,
  Little Jumping Joan;
Since Jesus is with me,
  I'm not all alone.

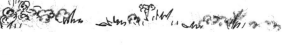

I HAD A LITTLE SYCAMORE TREE

I had a little sycamore tree,
  And what did I see in there?
A little man from Jericho
  Sat perched up in the air!
The King of Heaven's Great Son
  Stopped, and came to visit me;
And all for the sake
  Of the man up in my tree!

LITTLE BOY BLUE

Little Boy Blue,
  Come blow your horn,
The sheep's in the stable
  Where the Savior is born.
Where is the boy
  Who looks after the sheep?
Watching Baby Jesus,
  Fast asleep.

17

LITTLE BO-PEEP

Little Bo-Peep
  Has lost her sheep
And doesn't know where
  To find them;
But Jesus knows
  And can bring them home,
Wagging their tails behind them.

JESUS' FISHY BANK

There was a little fish
 In the Sea of Galilee,
Who played, and ate
 His seaweed greens,
As happy as can be.

Sometimes he peeped at people,
 And kept quiet as a mouse,
As he wondered what they did up there
 Upon the rooftop of his house.

19

They seemed to ride across it,
  In boats and nets of string;
And when he listened carefully,
  Sometimes he heard them sing...

"Jesus loves the little children,
All the children of the world,
Jesus loves the little children,
All the children of the world."

And that's how he learned of Jesus,
  From the men who sang and fished.
"I wish someday He'd talk to me,"
  His little fish heart just wished.

And then one sunny afternoon,
  When little fishes jump about,
A sparkling, golden coin
  Dropped...Plop!...
Upon his shimmering snout.

A sweet, kind voice said,
  "Little fish,
I've something for you to do.
  Please be a fishy bank for Me,
'Til My friend, Peter, calls on you."

20

The little fish knew right away
  That it was Jesus up there;
So he held on tightly to the coin
  And said, "I'll take good care."
Then Peter came in a day or two,
  For Jesus sent him down,
To reach into the waters blue
  And find that half-a-crown.

The little fish was waiting
  With the coin so faithfully.
And because he was a fishy bank for Jesus,
  He was the happiest fish in all the sea.

OLD MOTHER HUBBARD

Old Mother Hubbard
   Went to the cupboard,
To get her poor dog a bone;
   But when she got there
The cupboard was bare,
   And so the poor dog had none.

She went down the street
   Her good neighbors to meet,
And they all gathered round her in prayer;
   And when she got back,
She found bones in a sack
   Saying, "God wants us all to share!"

DING, DONG, BELL

Ding, dong, bell,
    There's gladness in the well!
Who put it in?
    God! It's genuine!
Who can get it out?
    Anyone who doesn't doubt.
Ding, dong, bell,
    There's gladness in the well!

LITTLE ROBIN REDBREAST

Little Robin Redbreast
  Sat upon a rail,
Niddle-naddle went his head,
  Wiggle-waggle went his tail.

Little Robin Redbreast
  Sang upon a rail,
"Thank You, Lord," went his head,
  "Praise You!" went his tail!

ONCE I SAW A LITTLE WORD

Once I saw a little word
  Come hop, hop, hop;
It wasn't kind at all,
  And I cried, "Stop, stop, stop!"

Once I saw a little word
  As soft as heather;
I blew it through my lips
  And said, "Go on forever!"

BOW, WOW, WOW

Bow, wow, wow,
  Whose dog art thou?
Little Tom Tinker's dog,
  Bow, wow, wow.

Bow, wow, wow,
  Who madest thou?
Little Tom Tinker's God!
  Bow, wow, wow.

GO TO
BED LATE

Go to bed late,
  Stay very small;
Go to bed early,
  Grow very tall.

Seek the Lord late,
  Treasures are small;
Seek the Lord early,
  Treasures are tall.

ROCK-A-BYE, BABY

Rock-a-bye, baby,
  On the tree top,
When the wind blows
  The cradle will rock;
Mother will make
  The baby a shawl;
God will keep baby,
  Cradle and all.

26

HICKETY, PICKETY,
MY BLACK HEN

Hickety, pickety, my black hen,
She lays eggs with quill and pen;
Gentlemen come every day
To see what my black hen's eggs say.

Some say, "Ask,"
Some say, "Given,"
Some say, "Come — and be not driven."
Some say, "Seek,"
Some say, "Find,"
Some say, "Leaving things behind."
Some say, "Coming back again,"
Hickety, pickety, my black hen.

PAT-A-CAKE

Pat-a-cake, pat-a-cake,
　Baker's man,
Bake me a cake
　As fast as you can.
Pat it and prick it,
　And mark it with G,
Put it in the oven
　For God and me.

BAA, BAA, BLACK SHEEP

Baa, baa, black sheep.
　Have you any wool?
Yes, sir, yes, sir,
　Three bags full:
One for my master,
　One for the Lord, too,
And one for the little boy
　Who says, "Thank you!"

GOOSEY, GOOSEY, GANDER

Goosey, goosey, gander,
   Where do you wander?
Upstairs and downstairs
   To watch, and to ponder
All the little children
   Saying Good Night Prayers,
And see their mommies kiss them,
   Then tip-toe down the stairs.

FEE, FI, FO, FUM

Fee, fi, fo, fum,
   I smell cookies
That smell yum-yum.
   Be they oatmeal
Or gingerbread,
   Before I eat them
I'll bow my head.

IF

If all the world were paper
   And seas were ink so blue,
We couldn't write enough to tell
   How much that God loves you.

29

A BLESSING ON YOUR HEAD

A blessing on your head,
A blessing on your toe;
A blessing, little one,
To keep you safe
Where'er you go.

A blessing on your nose,
A blessing on your ears;
A blessing, little one,
To keep you happy
Through the years.

A blessing on your lips,
A blessing on your eyes;
A blessing, little one,
To help you grow
Like Jesus—wise!

A blessing on your hands,
A blessing on your days;
A blessing now
To bless the Lord,
With little hearts of praise!

30

RING-A-RING O' ROSES

Ring-a-ring o' roses,
　　A pocket full of posies,
It's true! It's true!
　　Jesus rose for me and you!

Ring-a-ring o' roses,
　　A pocket full of posies,
It's true! It's true!
　　He's coming back for me and you!

SIX LITTLE MICE SAT DOWN TO SPIN

Six little mice
Sat down to spin,
Six little days
To work therein.

One day for spinning…
   The wheel went, "Plack, Plack,"
One day for weaving…
   The loom went, "Clack, Clack,"
One day for cutting…
   With scissors, "Snip, Snip,"
One day for sewing…
   With needles, "Nip, Nip,"
One day for fitting…
   The mice cried, "OO-OO!"
One day for pressing…
   With irons, "Scoo, Scoo."

Six little mice
Sat down to spin,
Six little days
To work therein.

Six little mice dressed in cotton and cord,
Finished in time for the day of the Lord!

IPSEY WIPSEY SPIDER

Ipsey Wipsey Spider,
  Climbing up the spout.
Little Miss Muffet said,
  "Keep on—don't doubt!"
Ipsey Wipsey Spider
  One foot at a time,
Reached the tip-top
  In the bright sunshine!

JACK BE NIMBLE

Jack be nimble,
  Jack be quick,
To bring your Mommy
  A flower you've picked.

LITTLE TOMMY TITTLEMOUSE

Little Tommy Tittlemouse
  Lived in a little house,
Built on a Rock
  That would stand, stand, stand.

Little Danny Dormouse
  Lived in a storehouse,
Built on a mound
  Of sand, sand, sand.

Then the rains came like a flood!
Which house do you think stood?

Crash! Bash! Danny's fell!
  Tommy's stayed up very well!

DANDELION SEA

Once upon a time
　　There was a happy little place
Called Dandelion Sea,
　　Where tiny bugs
And leaping frogs
　　Lived together, joyfully.

They had shops and streets,
　　And birthday treats,
Like little girls and boys;
　　And Grandpa Mole
At the edge of the pond
　　Made them whistles, flutes and toys.

GRANDPA
MOLE

Charlie Cricket was the mailman,
  Who jumped from house to house,
Chirping, "Good day!"
  To all his friends,
And taking cheese to Mrs. Mouse.

Barney Beetle was the baker,
  Baking nutty, whole-wheat bread.
"Indeed, it was the most scrumptious loaf
  I've ever eaten," Robin Redbreast said.

When the sun went down
  Each night about eight,
Then the band in the town would meet;
  And the little lightning bugs would bring
Their lights to lighten each street.

The ladybugs played violins,
  And the beetles banged their drums,
The frogs and toads played bass guitars,
  And the hummingbirds all hummed.

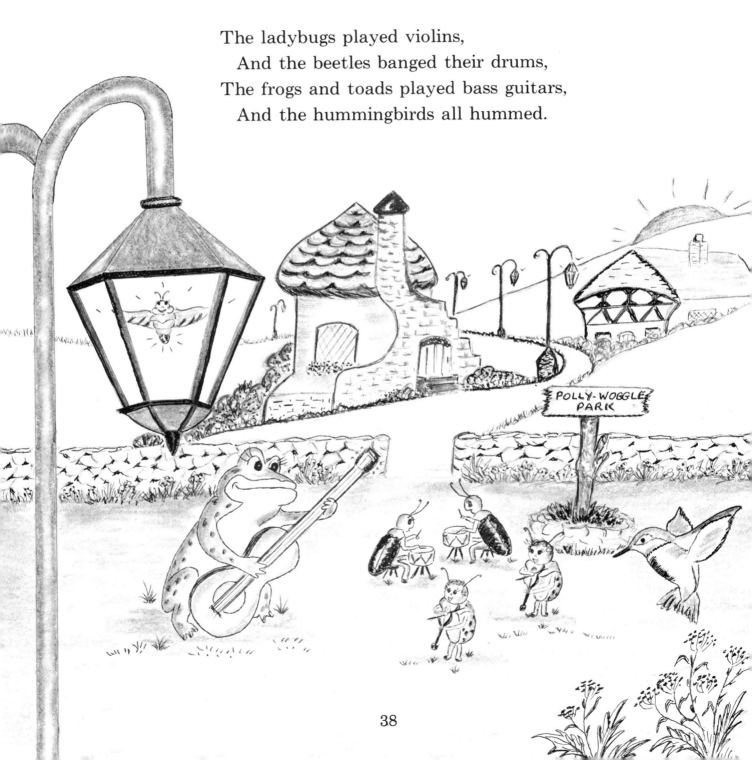

But best of all
    Was the end of the week,
When Sammy Sparrow would ring
    The church bell.
And then the whole town
    Of Dandelion Sea
Would listen to Rabbit tell
    How God made all the creatures great,
And creatures very small,
    And made a home for all of them
Because He loves them all.

JACK AND JILL

Jack and Jill
   Went up the hill
To fetch a pail of water.
   A man there said,
"If you drink this,
   You'll still be thirsty after."

"But there is water Jesus gives,
  So won't you ask Him first,
To give you LIVING WATER
  So that you will never thirst."

Up Jack got
  And home did trot,
A whole mile and a quarter,
  To tell the GOOD NEWS
To his friends,
  About God's LIVING WATER.

LAVENDER'S BLUE, DILLY, DILLY

Lavender's blue, dilly, dilly,
   Lavender's green,
Teach me to say, dilly, dilly,
   John 3:16.
God loved the world, dilly, dilly,
   He gave His son,
To give His life, dilly, dilly,
   For everyone.

Lavender's blue, dilly, dilly,
   Lavender's green,
Here comes the King, dilly, dilly,
   In clouds He's seen.
I'll wear my best, dilly, dilly,
   My whitest gown,
The King will give, dilly, dilly,
   To me a crown.

BLESS MY LITTLE FRIENDS

Bless my little friends, dear Jesus,
 Bless the people everywhere.
Bless my puppy, bless my cat,
 And bless my little rocking chair.

HICKORY, DICKORY, DOCK

Hickory, dickory, dock,
 The church mouse ran up the clock.
The clock struck ten,
 The mouse said, "Amen,"
 Hickory, dickory, dock.

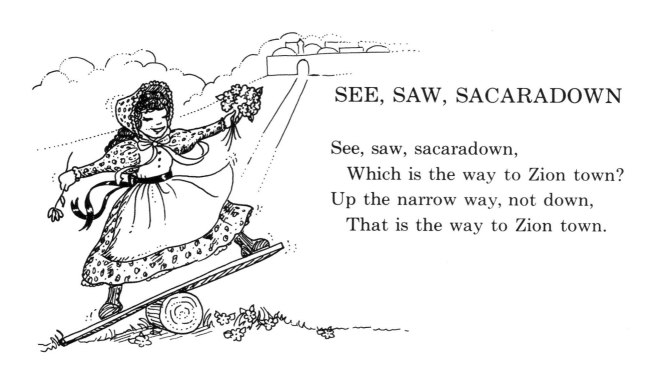

SEE, SAW, SACARADOWN

See, saw, sacaradown,
  Which is the way to Zion town?
Up the narrow way, not down,
  That is the way to Zion town.

LITTLE JACK HORNER

Little Jack Horner
  Sat in a corner,
Reading his Bible each day;
  He learned what it said,
And each night in bed,
  The verses he learned he would say.

The first night he said:
  "Since God so loved us
  We should love one another."
The next night he said:
  "Obey Father and Mother."
At the end of the week
  He had learned verse seven,
That Jesus is the way to Heaven.

MISTRESS MARY

Mistress Mary, quite contrary,
  How does your garden grow?
God sends rain and sun,
  And then one by one
The flowers pop up in a row.

I CAN'T SEE THE WIND

I can't see the wind,
   But I see what it blows:
Balloons in the air
   And Mommy's washed clothes.
I can't see God's Spirit
   Blowing down from above,
But I see how He blows
   Our home full of His love.

THE OLD WOMAN
IN A BASKET

There was an old woman
    Tossed up in a basket,
Nineteen times as high as the moon.
    And where she was going
I couldn't but ask it,
    For she was saying,
"I must find the way soon!"

"Old woman, old woman,
    Old woman," said I,
"Where are you flying
    Up so high?"
"To find heaven's door,"
    She said with a sigh.

"Oh, come back down,
    I'll show you," said I.
"Here is the Door,
    It's not in the sky.
The Door is dear Jesus,
    And He hears your cry,
HE'LL take you to heaven,
    By and By."

46

LUCY LOCKET

Lucy Locket lost her pocket,
Kitty Fisher found it;
She was honest,
So she took it back
With ribbon round it.

LITTLE TOMMY TUCKER

Little Tommy Tucker
  Sang for his supper.
What was the song
  That he sang
For bread and butter?

"God is so good,
  And God cares for little Tom."

That's what he sang
  Down to the last crumb.

IF I'D AS MUCH MONEY AS I COULD SPEND

If I'd as much money as I could spend,
    I never a broken heart could mend;
I never could buy the snow to send,
    Or buy a trip to the rainbow's end,
If I'd as much money as I could spend.

If I'd as much money as I could tell,
   I never could make a cockle shell;
I never could stay the spring's farewell,
   Or store the tide to buy and sell,
If I'd as much money as I could tell.

If I'd as much money from Pole to Pole,
   I never could buy my friend's dear soul,
For only Jesus can make us whole,
   And write our names on Heaven's scroll;
      And HE ever could!
      Oh, HE ever would
      Do all these things,
      Kindly and free,
      Out of His love
      For you and me.

HEY DIDDLE DINKETY,
POPPETY, PET

Hey diddle dinkety, poppety, pet,
   The merchants of London
Have formed a quartet!
   Wearing their garments
Of praise, hat to hem,
   So merrily sing the merchant men!

THE RAIN FOREST

The rain forest is
   The most pleasant place yet,
Especially for creatures
   Who like to get wet.

And even the ones
   Who like to stay dry,
Will drop in to see
   What goes on passing by.

The rain that falls there
   Is not usual rain;
When it falls, things will happen
   No one can explain.

Nothing-Impossible-Possum
   Lives near,
And watches for signs
   Of the rain to appear.

One of the signs
   Is a great weather vane,
That spins seven times
   At the coming of rain!

Nothing-Impossible-Possum
   Can tell
Wonderful tales,
   Of the forest's wet spell.

51

For the rain forest clouds
    Are not dark and drear,
But hold rainbow-rain
    That drops crystally-clear.

Nothing-Impossible-Possum
    Looks out,
To keep careful watch
    As a rainbow-rain scout.

The moment he sees
    The weather vane spin,
He blows on his flute
    A quick news bulletin.

RAIN FOREST

WATCH FOR FORMER AND LATTER RAINS
♥ BLESSINGS WHEN WET ♥
NOTHING-IMPOSSIBLE-POSSUM, RAINBOW RAIN SCOUT
BY APPOINTMENT OF HIS MAJESTY

"The rain is coming,
    The rainbow-rain!
Leave what you're doing,
    Don't stop to explain.

Bring all the children!
    Such wonders to see,
Out in the rain
    'Neath a rain forest tree."

Then down comes the rain!
    And through each lovely drop,
Your eyes can see under,
    Instead of on top!

Inside of tree trunks,
    Right down to the root,
You'll see little seeds
    Dressing up to be fruit!

52

You can see how the soil
　　Drinks up the soft rain,
To help push up flowers,
　　And long stalks of grain.

The small clumps of herbs,
　　At the first drops that fall,
Sprout into a garden
　　Exceedingly tall!

The rain magnifies
　　Everything you see in it;
That's why you can see
　　The whole land in a minute!

Nothing-Impossible-Possum
　　Said he
Saw small drops of rain
　　That turned into a sea!

Then saw the great sea
　　Become a great ocean,
From little rain showers
　　Joined merry, in motion.

Nothing-Impossible-Possum's
　　In tune
With the news of the greatest
　　Of rains—coming soon!

And what will it bring?
　　Well, it's written, no doubt;
So watch for the bright clouds
　　To rain, and find out!

53

DAFFY-DOWN-DILLY

Daffy-Down-Dilly
Has come to town,
In a yellow petticoat
And a green gown.

"Did you work very hard
   To spin cloth by the yard?"
Said a blue-bird to Daffy-Down-Dilly.

"I must really confess
   It's a dazzling dress,"
Said a frog from a pink water-lily.

"How much dye did it take,
   Such bright yellow to make?"
Said a honeybee in the blue heather.

"Tell me, how did you grow?
   Then your secret I'll know,"
Said the wise owl with pen of brown feather.

"No! I did not work hard
To spin cloth by the yard;
And I did not buy dye for this yellow.
As to how I did grow…
Please consider this, so
You can learn of my secret, good fellow:

Where God placed me
  I grew!
In the spot
  Where He knew
Was the best
  For a Daffy-Down-Dilly.
So I stayed
  Rooted there,
And with His
  Loving care
I bloomed into
  A beautiful lily!"

"Consider that, now!"
  Said the wise old owl;
"I must write it down
  With my brown feather."
"Consider that, now!"
  Said the bird, frog and bee,
And they all considered together,
      HOW...
Daffy-Down-Dilly
  Had come to town,
    In a yellow petticoat
      And a green gown!

57

HERE WE GO ROUND THE MIRACLE BUSH

Here we go round the miracle bush,
   The miracle bush, the miracle bush;
Here we go round the miracle bush,
   We go around like Moses.

Take off our shoes, it's holy ground,
   Holy ground, it's holy ground;
Take off our shoes, it's holy ground,
   Take off our shoes like Moses.

Obey the Lord as Moses did,
   Moses did, as Moses did;
Obey the Lord as Moses did,
   Obey the Lord like Moses.

WHEN I LOOK UP AT A STAR

When I look up at a star,
  I know it's very, very far.
When I look up at the sky,
  I know it's very, very high.

When I try to find the sea,
  I know it's very far from me.
When I see a mountain tall,
  I know I'm very, very small.

But when I look to God on high,
  Who lives beyond the starry sky,
I know that He will always be
  Very, very close to me.

MOLLY, MY SISTER, AND I

Molly, my sister,
  And I fell out,
And what do you think
  It was all about?
Her skirt was long,
  Mine came to the knee;
And that was the reason
  We couldn't agree!

Molly, my sister,
  And I fell out,
But what do you think
  Turned us round about?
I loved her,
  And she loved me;
And that was the reason
  We could agree!

BLOW, WIND, BLOW

Blow, wind, blow!
  Go, mill, go!
Go by the four winds together;
  Breathe on the valley
That's very dry,
  Bring in the corn
And the wheat and rye.
  Blow, wind, blow!
Go, mill, go!
  Go by the four winds together.

61

HOW MANY MILES TO BETHLEHEM?

How many miles to Bethlehem?
  Three score miles and ten.
Can I get there by candlelight?
  Yes, and back again.

How many miles to Heaven?
  More than three score and ten.
Can I get there by Daystar-light?
  Yes, and back again!

OLD KING COLE

Old King Cole
Was a merry old soul,
And a merry old soul was he;
He called for the Lord
To save his soul,
And he called for his fiddlers three.

Every fiddler
Had a fine fiddle,
And a fine fiddle ministry;
Oh, for song and prayer
None can compare
With King Cole and his fiddlers three!

THE NOTHING-IMPOSSIBLE-POSSUM

Have you heard of the
　　Nothing-Impossible-Possum,
Who dreamed of a flute
　　Made of pink apple blossom?

And not just a flute
　　That *one* possum could blow,
But a flute that would toot
　　'Round the world in one go!

And not just a flute
　　With one toot blown each day,
But a flute that would toot
　　Morning, night in relay!

And not just a flute
　　Blown at morning and night,
But a flute that would toot
　　Every second in sight!

64

And not just a flute
  That each second would sound;
But a flute that would toot
  Every musical sound!

Low notes
And high notes,
And in-between shy notes;
And notes that would whistle and woo.
SING sounds,
And ZING sounds,
And echoing PING sounds,
And sounds ringing FOO-FEE-A-ROO!

65

Trill tunes
And hill tunes,
And happy-goodwill tunes;
And tunes to astound and amaze!
Whirled songs
And twirled songs,
And all-cross-the-world songs,
And songs everywhere in God's praise!

"It's really absurd,"
   Said a glum mockingbird,
"To be playing a flute night and day.
   Who would listen that long
   To a possum's flute song?
Take your dreams, sir, and throw them away."

"It's a possible dream,
   And I'll stay with my scheme,"
Said the Nothing-Impossible-Possum;
 "And a big flute brigade
   Will praise God in parade;
And I'll start with this pink apple blossom!"

So he carved out a flute
  That one possum could blow,
Then asked his good friend
  If he'd join on below.

His friend, the raccoon,
  Took a nice maple limb,
And soon shaped a flute
  To join onto the rim.

So sitting together
  They warbled a tune,
Which brought out a beaver
  Who knew the raccoon.

"I'm an expert with wood!
  If you fellows don't mind,
I'll join on my flute,
  Then we'll all play combined."

The three played together
  And woke up a rabbit,
Who said, "I'll be part
  Of this musical habit."

So now four were playing —
  The flute was quite long,
When up walked a duck
  Who joined in with the song.

"Come! Bring an extension,
  We've a long way to go,"
They all told the duck,
  So *he* joined on to blow!

They blew songs of praise
  With such sounds never heard,
That for miles through the forest
  They shocked every bird!

Soon everyone wanted
   To join on the flute;
With a piece here and there
   It stretched miles with each toot!

It went through the forest
   And over the hills,
With PING sounds and ZING sounds,
   And sounds full of trills.

Across the great mountains,
   And 'round river bends;
With each creature adding,
   The flute could not end!

It reached the North Pole,
   Where a big polar bear
Said, "I've enough breath
   To blow ten miles from here!"

70

So he lengthened the flute
    For ten miles 'cross the ice,
Where two penguins cried,
    "What a marvelous device!"

"Is this what is making
    Such music each day?
We'd like to join in
    And praise God, if we may."

"If God gave you breath,
    Then you're part of our throng,"
The polar bear smiled,
    "Come and join in our song."

71

Then down from the North Pole
  Came low notes and high;
The flute ever growing,
  With each passerby.

Creatures with long necks,
  And some with big snouts,
All happily blowing
  And praising with shouts!

Behold! Every second
  Of each night and day,
A round-the-world flute
  Toot-toot-tooted in play!

Low notes
And high notes,
And in-between shy notes;
And notes that would whistle and woo.
SING sounds,
And ZING sounds,
And echoing PING sounds,
And sounds ringing FOO-FEE-A-ROO!

Trill tunes
And hill tunes,
And happy-goodwill tunes;
And tunes to astound and amaze!
Whirled songs,
And twirled songs,
And all-cross-the-world songs,
And songs everywhere in God's praise!

And how did it start?
   With a pink apple blossom!
And the dream of that
   Nothing-Impossible-Possum!

GRANDMA AND ME

Grandma told me
  She used to be
A little girl
  Who looked like me.

She had a big,
  Brown teddy bear,
And a cuddly doll
  With golden hair.

She told me
  That she used to pray,
And thank God
  For her food each day.

And one day
  When she was just seven,
Her daddy told her
  The way to Heaven.

And on that birthday
  Long ago,
She told the Lord
  She loved Him so.

And now that I
  Am nearly seven,
She told me, too,
  God's way to Heaven.

Oh, I believe
  What Grandma said.
Her Bible she has
  Read and read.

And she is good
  And kind to me,
As God wants all
  Grandmas to be.

SEE-SAW, MARGERY DAW

See-saw, Margery Daw,
  Jackie has found a new Master.
His Name is Jesus, Shepherd and Friend,
  And Jackie's a sheep in His pasture.

LITTLE MISS MUFFET

Little Miss Muffet
  Sat on a tuffet,
Thanking Jesus for curds and whey;
  There came a big spider
And sat down beside her,
  To listen to Miss Muffet pray.

She said...

"Thank you, Lord Jesus,
For good things to eat.
　For berries and nuts
And apples, so sweet.
　I really can't see
How you feed this big world;
　The lions and tigers
And pigs with tails curled.
　The puppies and rabbits,
The birds in the air,
　The horses and cows,
You give them a fair share.
　The sheep and the cats
On your food they dine;
　So thank you, Lord Jesus,
For my kitty's food and mine."

Little Miss Muffet
　Sat on a tuffet,
Thanking Jesus
　For curds and whey;
And then that big spider
　Who listened beside her,
Knelt down with Miss Muffet to pray.

ONE MISTY, MOISTY MORNING

One misty, moisty morning,
When cloudy was the weather,
There I met an old man
Clothed all in leather.
I put my hand beneath his arm
And helped him through the rain.
He said, "I thank you, thank you, child,
And thank you, once again."

BOBBY SHAFTOE

Bobby Shaftoe's gone to sea,
To pray upon his little knee
That boys and girls will come to see
That Jesus really loves them.

Bobby Shaftoe's kind and good,
He helps his daddy bring in wood;
He obeys Mother, as he should,
Happy Bobby Shaftoe.

HOW PRAISE SAVED
BENJAMIN BUMBLEBEE

One sunny summer morning,
  In Dandelion Sea,
As Charlie Cricket delivered mail
  He heard a voice say, cheerily…

"Hello, there, Mr. Mailman,
  Is this Dandelion Sea?
I just flew in to get some help
  For Benjamin Bumblebee."

"He's lost inside a pipe organ
  And can't find his way out;
The noise he's making down in there
  Is booming out each spout!"

"The pipe organ is in a church
  In Dippley Dockerlee,
And when Benjamin came visiting
  He flew down Pipe Number Fifty-Three!"

"He kept five towns awake last night
  With his buzzing in those pipes.
And I heard him say, 'Please get some help,
  I've nearly buzzed off all my stripes.' "

"Poor Benjamin! He needs us,"
  Charlie said. "I'll take a stand.
But may I ask your name, sir,
  And if you'll shake my hand?"

"Oh, please forgive me, Charlie!
  Of course, you wonder who I must be.
Well…my name is Dippley Dock
  And I'm from Dippley Dockerlee."

"In Dippley Dockerlee
  We have flocks and flocks and flocks,
Of roly-poly Docker bugs
  Which sound like little clocks."

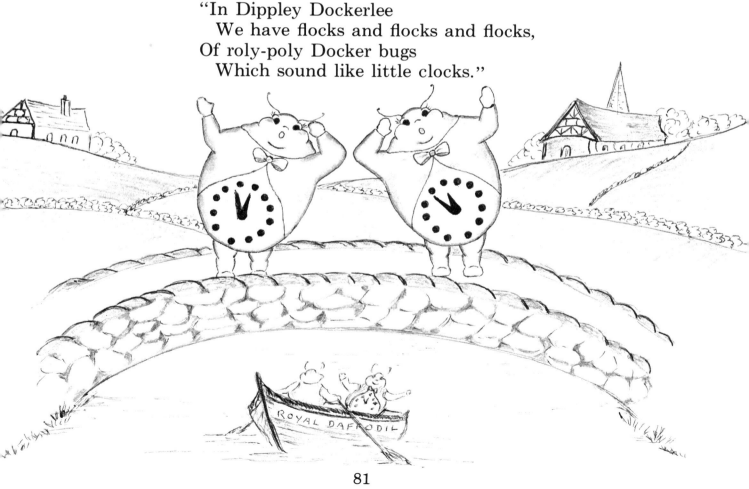

"But now we can't hear ourselves tick
   In Dippley Dockerlee,
Because of all that booming noise
   From Benjamin Bumblebee!"

Charlie said, "What can we do?
   What can be quickly sent,
So that Benjamin can find his way
   Out of that instrument?"

"Well, Charlie, we've done all we can
   To find him in two days,
But still we haven't got him out;
   I think we should try Praise!"

"The Bible says we should praise God,
   For praising brings His power.
In everything we should give thanks;
   Let's start this very hour!"

So Charlie Cricket and Dippley Dock
   Told Brother Rabbit right away,
"Tell everyone and everything
   To praise for Benjamin today."

Then soon within that very hour
    The news went everywhere;
And clouds of sounds of praising God
    Went floating in the air…WITH…

Bees a-buzzing,
Butterflies flitting,
Grasshoppers hopping,
Frogs a-jumping,
Roosters crowing,
Spiders swinging,
Birds a-singing
    "PRAISE THE LORD!"

Dogs a-barking,
Sheep a-bleating,
Donkeys braying,
Cows a-mooing,
Squirrels chattering,
Hens a-cackling,
Ducks a-quacking
    "PRAISE THE LORD!"

Geese a-honking,
Turkeys gobbling,
Cats meowing,
Pigs a-grunting,
Crickets chirruping,
Chipmunks cheeping,
Mice a-squeaking
   "PRAISE THE LORD!"

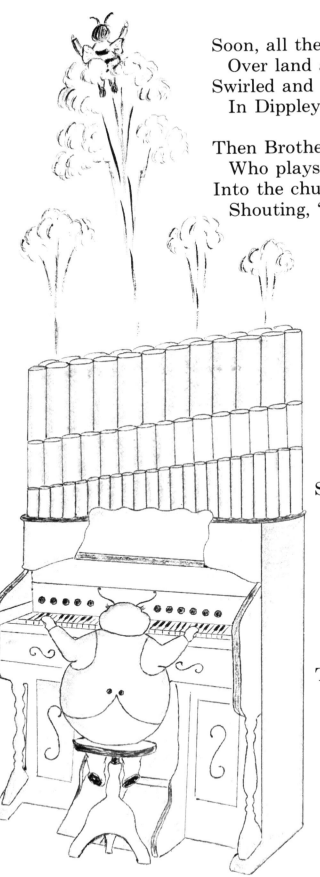

Soon, all the sounds of praise and praise
  Over land and over sea,
Swirled and twirled around the church
  In Dippley Dockerlee!

Then Brother Davey Docker
  Who plays the organ, flew
Into the church at double-tick,
  Shouting, "I'll join in, too!"

He sat down at the organ
  And pumped without a doubt;
And as he played,
  "Let's Praise The Lord,"
    He blew Benjamin…
    SWOOSH!…RIGHT OUT!

So……….
  Praising God together
  Is what saved our little friend,
  And Benjamin would like to tell you
  To praise God from beginning to end!

    BUZZ-A-BUZZ-BUZZ…
    BUZZ-A-BUZZ-BUZZ…

That's Benjamin saying,
  "PRAISE THE LORD!
    GOODBYE!"

86

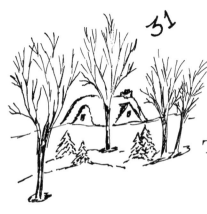

THE MONTHS RHYME

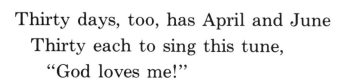

Thirty days hath September,
  Thirty days to remember,
    God loves you!

Thirty days, too, has April and June
  Thirty each to sing this tune,
    "God loves me!"

Thirty days hath November,
  Thirty days to remember
    God loves you!

January, March, July and May
  Have thirty-one days for you to say,
    "We love Him!"

August, October and December
  Have thirty-one days to remember,
    God loves you!

February only has twenty-eight,
  Twenty-eight days for you to state,
    "We love Him!"

But in Leap Year there's some extra time,
  When February then has twenty-nine,
    Twenty-nine days to remember,
      God loves you!

SMILE AT YOUR ANGEL

Did you know
  That there are angels
Standing by you?
  Yes! It's so!
And although you cannot see them,
  They go everywhere you go.
They will watch you at the table,
  They will watch at night in bed;
They will watch when you are playing;
  They hear everything that's said.
So, when you wake up in the morning
  And look out at the sky,
Smile and say, "Good morning!"
  To your angel standing by.

WHEN DADDY PRAYS FOR ME

If I fall down and scrape my knee,
  I ask Daddy to pray for me.
It makes me feel so good and fine
  When his big hands fold over mine.
Or when he puts them on my head
  Before I jump into my bed.
I know that everything will be
  All right, when Daddy prays for me.

88

WEE WILLIE WINKIE

Wee Willie Winkie
 Runs through the town,
Upstairs and downstairs
 In his nightgown;
Rapping at the windows,
 Shouting through the locks,
"Have the children
 Said their prayers?
It's past eight o'clock!"

Wee Willie Winkie
 Runs through the town,
Asking moms and daddies
 In his nightgown,
"Did you tuck the children in
 And listen while they pray;
And ask the Lord to bless them
 Through the night and through the day?"

WOULD YOU PRAISE HIM ON A CACTUS?

Would you praise Him
  On a cactus?
Would you praise Him
  Just for practice?

Would you praise Him
  In a hole?
Would you praise Him
  On a pole?

Would you praise Him
  When you're small?
Would you praise Him
  When you're tall?

DANDELION
SEA

Would you praise Him
In a tree?
Would you praise Him
On your knee?

Would you praise Him
On a roof?
Would you praise Him
With one tooth?

Would you praise Him
With a song?
Would you praise Him
With a gong?

Would you praise Him
  In old shoes?
Would you praise Him
  When you lose?

Would you praise Him
  Beating drums?
Would you praise Him
  With smashed thumbs?

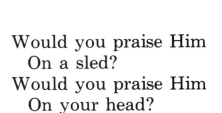

Would you praise Him
  On a sled?
Would you praise Him
  On your head?

Would you praise Him
   In a pew?
Would you praise Him
   In an igloo?

Would you praise Him
   With a clown?
Would you praise Him
   Round the town?

Would you praise Him
   When you're glad?
Would you praise Him
   When you're sad?

Would you praise Him
Blowing bubbles?
Would you praise Him
In your troubles?

Would you praise Him
With a dove?
Would you praise Him
For His love?

Would you praise Him
Hot or cooler?
YES! I'LL PRAISE HIM!
HALLELUJAH!

I HAD A LITTLE PONY

I had a little pony,
   His name was Dapple Gray.
I lent him to the Lord to ride
   Down into town, one day.
Jesus patted him and rode him,
   And people waved palm limbs.
Oh, I'd lend my pony any time
   That Jesus needed him!

SING A SONG OF SIXPENCE

Sing a song of sixpence,
   A pocket for the Lord;
Four and twenty children
   A penny could afford
To send across the ocean,
   For other children there
To learn about dear Jesus,
   Who answers every prayer.

JOSH'S 5,000 LUNCHES

Once upon a time
   There was a little boy named Josh.
He liked to go out fishing
   And splash and splush and splosh.

One day he took his pole,
   And his mother made a lunch,
Because young boys who fish and play
   Need something to munch and crunch.

Josh chased the little fishes
   Under rocks and down the stream,
But couldn't catch even one,
   As easy as that may seem!

He walked along the stream
  Making frizby-frozby noise,
But little fishes hide away
  From splashing, sploshing boys.

He sang, "Oh, Frizby and Frozby,
  I'll catch you if I can;
You cannot hide from me,
  For I'm a great fisherman."

He soon was tired and hungry,
  And said to those hiding fish,
"If you come up, I'll share my lunch,
  Five loaves and two little fish."

"Five loaves and two little fish
  You'll share?" a man said, suddenly;
"You're just the boy that Jesus needs.
  I'm Andrew—do come with me."

So little Josh jumped up
  And ran with Andrew on tip-toe,
Up to the hill where Jesus stood,
  With five thousand people below.

"Here's a boy, Lord Jesus,
  With a lunch of fish and bread.
Josh, would you give your lunch to Jesus
  To make five thousand lunches instead?"

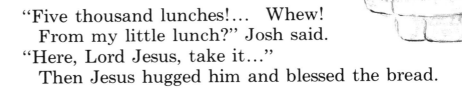

"Five thousand lunches!... Whew!
  From my little lunch?" Josh said.
"Here, Lord Jesus, take it..."
  Then Jesus hugged him and blessed the bread.

One...two...and a hundred,
  The lunch kept making more and more,
As Jesus passed it from His hands...
  Four thousand and forty-four!

At last 5,000 hungry people
  All ate their lunch that day,
From two little fish and five little loaves
  That Josh had given away.

Josh ran home so excited,
  He forgot to splash and splush.
The hiding fishes in the stream
  Said, "Josh is in such a rush!"

They heard him say, "Oh Frizby
  And oh, Frozby, you can hide;
I went fishing with Jesus today
  And my lunch was multiplied!"

Then he remembered his dear mommy
  Had packed the fish and bread,
So she had also helped the Lord
  And people who were fed.

"Oh, Mommy, Mommy!" he cried out,
  "When you made my lunch today,
You were really making 5,000 lunches
  For Jesus to give away!"

GRANDPA MOLE'S PARTY

"Hello children!

I'm knocking on the door of a strange little house.

It's down in the ground, under a big tree by the pond in Dandelion Sea.

It's Grandpa Mole's house!

He invited all of us to a party today. He loves to have parties for his dear friends. You are a dear friend of his and so am I!"

GRANDPA MOLE

Knock – knock – knock…ring-a-ling!…

"He must be very busy, so we'll ring again."

Ring-a-ling!…

"Boys and girls, will you help me call him?
I'm sure he'll hear if we both call out,
Grandpa Mole! We're here!"

"Thank you! Here he comes."

"Sorrabahum…Sorrabahum…"

(Remember, boys and girls, that's how
Grandpa Mole says, "Bless you, children.")

"Bless you, too, Grandpa Mole.
Thank you for inviting us to your party."

"What a cozy little house you have
All green and brown and red.
And a fireplace with an oven
Baking bingle-berry bread!"

Hmmmmm…fruits and nuts
And honey cones
For Benjamin Bumblebee.
And dandelion dandies
For Charlie Cricket, I see.

Well…here is Charlie now.
" Hello, Charlie…do come in!"
"Chirrup, chirrup, chirrup,
I've brought Lucy Ladybug's violin."

Here comes Lucy with Mrs. Mouse!
And Barney Beetle's bringing a cake.
Sammy and Mrs. Sparrow
Just flew in from Lily-pad Lake.

Luke and Larry Lightning Bug
Are lighting up the lamp.
And here is Benjamin Bumblebee
Buzzing in from Honeyrock Camp.

Hippity, Hoppity…Here's Brother Rabbit,
Now everyone is here.
"But what's that extra place for,
Grandpa Mole, and that special chair?"

"That place is set for Jesus,
We want Him to be our guest,
So we set a special place for Him,
Our very, very best!"

"Let's sing our prayer to thank Him
For bingle-berry bread."
"And dandelion dandies!"
Charlie Cricket said.

So we all sang together:

"Thank you, Lord, for bingle-berry bread,
  Bingle-berry bread,
  Bingle-berry bread.
Thank you, Lord, for bingle-berry bread,
  And for Grandpa Mole.
Come and be our special guest,
  Special guest, special guest.
Come and be our special guest,
  Lord Jesus, come, we pray."

And what a happy time everyone had!—
Singing, eating and playing games!

We all agreed that Grandpa Mole's house
Was one of the finest places in the whole world
To have a party.

Then Grandpa Mole said,
"I hope all of you wonderful girls and boys
Will have a special place for the Lord Jesus
At your next party."

"Sorrabahum.....Sorrabahum.....
Bless you, children."

"Bless you, too, dear Grandpa Mole,
And thank you for this lovely party!"

DID JESUS?

"Mommy," my Johnny asked one day,
  "When Jesus was a boy at play,
Did He chase a rabbit
  And catch a frog,
And did he have a little white dog?"

"Did He pick a daisy for His mommy dear?
  When he bumped His head,
Did He cry a tear?
  And when He was all tucked in bed,
  What were the stories
  His mommy read?
Did He sail a paper boat at sea,
  And do all those things...
  Just like me?"

105

"Did He help His daddy to cut some wood,
  And dig in the sand
As fast as He could?
  And when He looked up in the sky,
Did He wish to go up there and fly?
  Did He go out looking
  For a bird's nest?
Did He have to take a nap and rest?
  Did He love to climb up in a tree,
And do all those things...
  Just like me?"

"Yes, my Johnny,
  I'm sure it is true
That Jesus did all those things...
  Just like you."

RIDE A COCK-HORSE

Ride a cock-horse
  To Banbury Cross,
To see all the children
  Make music and sing.
With bells on their fingers
  And bells on each toe,
They praise God with music
  Wherever they go.

ONE, TWO, THREE, FOUR, FIVE

One, two, three, four, five,
  Once I caught a fish alive;
Six, seven, eight, nine, ten,
  Jesus said, "Now, fish for men!"
How can I catch men on a hook?
  God tells you how in His Good Book.

OLD MOTHER GOOSE

Old Mother Goose,
  When she wanted to wander,
Would ride through the air
  On a very fine gander.

She'd fly to a house
  That stood in the wood,
To tell all the children
  That God is so good.

And then she would sing them
   A bright, happy tune,
That Jesus is coming
   Back to the earth soon!
And children who love Him
   Are never alone,
And will see him as King
   On a beautiful throne.

Then off on her gander
   She'd fly through the air
To far away places,
   To tell children there.

Old Mother Goose,
   One fine morning, I'm told,
Will find up in Heaven
   Her house made of gold!

GRANDPA'S BIBLE

My Grandpa has a Bible
  That he keeps upon his table;
And when I grow big
  I'll open it
And read it...when I'm able.

When Mommy takes me visiting
  I climb on Grandpa's knee,
And he opens up the Bible
  So the pictures I can see.

There's a picture of Baby Moses
  In a basket, fast asleep.
And one of David carrying back home
  A little sheep.

There's a picture of a wooden ship
  With animals going in;
I like the tall giraffes and goats
  With whiskers on their chin.

HE WHO CUTS
HIS OWN WOOD
IS WARMED TWICE

There's a horse and chariot in the sky—
   That must be fun to ride!
And a picture of a big, big fish
   Which has a man inside.

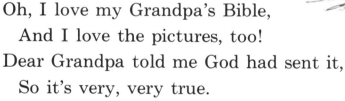

I saw a man in long, blue clothes
   Writing with a feather!
And lions with some baby lambs,
   All sleeping close together.

Most of all I like to see
   The boy who gave his bread
To Jesus, so that all the hungry
   People could be fed.

Oh, I love my Grandpa's Bible,
   And I love the pictures, too!
Dear Grandpa told me God had sent it,
   So it's very, very true.

Jesus came from Heaven
To love and help me,
   Yes, I know.
I know because
My Grandpa's Bible
   Told me so!

BENJAMIN BUMBLEBEE'S
ADVENTURE

A little drop of rain
  Fell in Dandelion Sea,
Right on the head
  Of Benjamin Bumblebee.

Now, Benjamin was gathering
  Some honey from a flower,
And said to himself,
  "Oh, it's just a little shower."

And then the sound of church bells
  Came ringing loud and clear,
And he knew that Sammy Sparrow
  Rang the bells for bees to hear.

He knew the bells were saying,
  "Fly quickly to Rabbit's umbrella;
Get underneath it or the rain
  Will wash you to Gopher's cellar!"

"I can take care of myself...I think...
    I don't need to hurry back ,"
Benjamin said, as he buzzed along;
    But the sky was turning black.

Then THREE BIG drops of rain
    Fell on Benjamin's small head;
And all at once, he was soaking wet.
    "I'd better get home!" he said.

But the big, black cloud then burst in two,
    And the rain made one big river.
And there was Benjamin floating away,
    All wet, all cold, all a-shiver.

"I wish I'd obeyed when I heard the bells,
    And flew to Rabbit's umbrella.
Everyone there is safe and dry,
    And I'm washing into a cellar!"

G. GOPHER
KEEP OUT!!

Now, back in town, in Dandelion Sea,
   Under Rabbit's red umbrella,
The other bees ate honey cones,
   Strawberry and vanilla.

"Where is Benjamin?" Rabbit said;
   "He must have stayed out in the rain.
He should be with us under cover,
   But he has disobeyed again!"

"I saw him in the clover field
   By Grouchy Gopher's place,"
Henry Honeybee spoke up,
   With honey cone on his face.

"Oh, dear! then he was washed away!—
   I must get Grandpa Mole
To rescue him before he drowns
   In Grouchy Gopher's hole."

So Rabbit ran to Grandpa Mole's
  To tell of Benjamin's plight.
"I'll go save him," Grandpa said,
  "But I need a bright flashlight."

"Take two lightning bugs with you
  And put one on each ear,"
Rabbit said."They will help you
  See the way more clear."

So Grandpa Mole, who swims so well,
  Went quietly down the stream,
With two bright lightning bugs
  Like headlights, lit up all agleam.

They went down under water,
  And followed Gopher's trench,
'Til they came into his cellar
  Where Benjamin was, all drenched!

He was bobbing in the water
  That had washed him underground,
Crying in his bumblebee tears,
  "I know I'll never be found!"

Just then, he saw the lights of
   Luke and Larry Lightning Bug,
And on Grandpa Mole's brown, tiny ears
   They gave a little tug.

"There he is!" they shouted,
   And lit up as bright as could be,
So that Grandpa Mole could see at once
   It was Benjamin Bumblebee.

Poor little Benjamin couldn't fly,
   He'd thought it was the end.
But here in Grouchy Gopher's cellar
   Had appeared his dearest friend.

Grandpa Mole then picked him up,
   Dripping wet and cold,
And placed him on his own warm nose
   And said, "You're safe inside my fold."

He swam so quietly out again,
    Luke and Larry on each ear,
And his nose out of the water,
    With Benjamin riding there.

At last they crossed the clover field
    And climbed back up the hill,
Where they could see that everyone
    Sat under cover still.

Right then, the sun came out so warm
    And dried off Benjamin's clothes.
"If you're feeling better," Grandpa said,
    "You can get down off my nose."

"Thank you, friend, for saving me
    From drowning in the cold.
I promise you, dear Grandpa Mole,
    That I'll now do as I'm told!"

117

Three days later...

A little drop of rain
 fell in Dandelion Sea,
Right on the head
 of Benjamin Bumblebee.
  BUZZZZ...
He flew back right away
 To Rabbit's red umbrella,
And while it rained
 Ate honey cones,
That happy little fella!

TWEEDLEDUM AND TWEEDLEDEE

Tweedledum and Tweedledee
  Once had a quarrel;
For Tweedledum said Tweedledee
  Had pushed him off a barrel.
Said Tweedledee to Tweedledum,
  "I'm very, very sorry."
Said Tweedledum to Tweedledee,
  "I'll forgive you in a hurry."

PETER, PETER

Peter, Peter, Simon Peter,
  Walked on water, totter-teeter.
At first he walked and teetered well,
  Then got afraid and—totter!—fell!
But Jesus reached out with His hand
  And brought him safely back to land.

THE LITTLE PUPPY AND JESUS

I'm just a little puppy
   Who gets under people's feet.
And one day a man called Jesus
   Came walking down our dusty street.

I nipped and bit His sandals,
   But He didn't shout at me.
He smiled and picked me up
   And stroked my back, so lovingly.

I felt so safe and happy
   Cuddled up inside His arm;
I knew it was the safest place
   In all the world, from harm.

And then He called me Fido;
   But how did He know my name?
There was no one there to tell Him,
   But He knew me, just the same.

We walked along together,
   And I licked Him on the chin.
He squeezed me closer to Him,
   And I think I saw Him grin!

At last we came to the seashore,
   By the Sea of Galilee,
And I fell asleep in the sunshine,
   Snuggled right upon His knee.

When I woke up and looked around,
  There were lots of girls and boys;
Jumping around and clapping hands,
  And making so much noise.

A man came along to chase them away,
  But Jesus said, "Let them be;
For I am the Friend of these children,
  So let them all come unto Me."

We had such a fine day together
  Jesus, the children and me;
And we played and sang and had some lunch,
  And splashed in the warm, blue sea.

Then came time for boys and girls
  To all go home, you see;
But I didn't have a home at all;
  So what would become of me?

I looked up at dear Jesus,
  To see what my Friend would do;
Then He picked me up and gave me to
  A fine little boy—just like you!

He said, "Take good care of Fido
  And treat him as your friend.
Give him food and water,
  And I will bless you, in the end."

I love that Man called Jesus,
  And I hope you love Him, too.
Because He loves little puppies like me,
  And, of course, boys and girls like you!

SING, SING

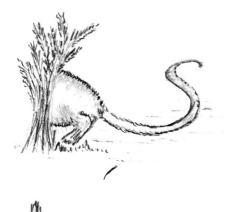

Sing, sing…
  What shall I sing?
The world is so full
  Of wonderful things!

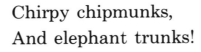

Snowballs and snails,
Long and short tails.

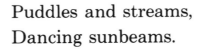

Chirpy chipmunks,
And elephant trunks!

Puddles and streams,
Dancing sunbeams.

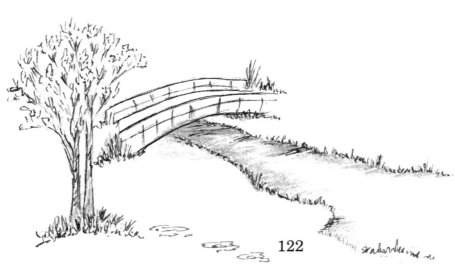

122

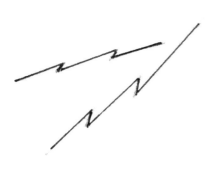

A camel's hump,
Grasshoppers that jump!

Pumpkins so big,
Sandcastles to dig.

Crabs folding under,
Lightning and thunder.

Clouds looking funny,
Bees making honey.

Sing, sing...
　I know what I'll sing!—

"God can make hundreds
　Of anything!"

THIS IS THE ARK
THAT NOAH BUILT

This is the Ark that Noah built.

This is the salt
That lay in the Ark
  That Noah built.

This is the goat,
That ate the salt
That lay in the Ark
  That Noah built.

This is the stoat,
That followed the goat,
That ate the salt
That lay in the Ark
  That Noah built.

124

This is the lamb,
That followed the stoat,
That followed the goat,
That ate the salt
That lay in the Ark
  That Noah built.

This is the ram,
That followed the lamb,
That followed the stoat,
That followed the goat,
That ate the salt
That lay in the Ark
  That Noah built.

This is the goose,
That followed the ram,
That followed the lamb,
That followed the stoat,
That followed the goat,
That ate the salt
That lay in the Ark
  That Noah built.

125

This is the moose,
That followed the goose,
That followed the ram,
That followed the lamb,
That followed the stoat,
That followed the goat,
That ate the salt
That lay in the Ark
  That Noah built.

This is the puppy,
All white and fluffy,
That followed the moose,
That followed the goose,
That followed the ram,
That followed the lamb,
That followed the stoat,
That followed the goat,
That ate the salt
That lay in the Ark
  That Noah built.

This is the cow,
That gave some milk
To feed the puppy,
All white and fluffy,
That followed the moose,
That followed the goose,
That followed the ram,
That followed the lamb,
That followed the stoat,
That followed the goat,
That ate the salt
That lay in the Ark
  That Noah built.

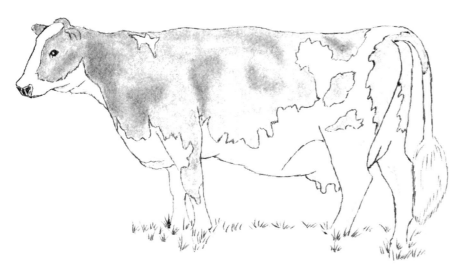

This is Noah's wife,
All dressed in silk,
Who milked the cow,
That gave some milk,
To feed the puppy,
All white and fluffy,
That followed the moose,
That followed the goose,
That followed the ram,
That followed the lamb,
That followed the stoat,
That followed the goat,
That ate the salt
That lay in the Ark
  That Noah built.

This is Noah,
As we've said before,
Who built the Ark
That saved his wife,
All dressed in silk,
Who milked the cow
That gave some milk,
To feed the puppy,
All white and fluffy,
That followed the moose,
That followed the goose,
That followed the ram,
That followed the lamb,
That followed the stoat,
That followed the goat,
That ate the salt
That lay in the Ark
  That Noah built.

This is the rain
That brought the flood
That covered the earth,
As God said it would;
And so called Noah,
As we've said before,
Who built the Ark
That saved his wife,
All dressed in silk,
Who milked the cow
That gave some milk,
To feed the puppy,
All white and fluffy,
That followed the moose,
That followed the goose,
That followed the ram,
That followed the lamb,
That followed the stoat,
That followed the goat,
That ate the salt
That lay in the Ark
    That Noah built.

This is the rainbow
In the sky,
That followed the Ark
When the earth was dry.
God gave the rainbow
That we should
Remember—
There'll never be a flood,
Like the one
When everything, two-by-two,
Went into the Ark
 That Noah built!

GOD MADE ME

Did you hear the robins singing,
　"God made me"?
And the crickets chirpy-chinging,
　"God made me."

Did you see the dandelions
　Blowing off their heads with glee?
And flying in the air shouting,
　"God made me!"

Don't you see the trees all swaying,
　Keeping time so prettily;
While bumblebees and beetles
　Sing together, "God made me."

Oh, look at the glowworms glowing,
　Flashing sparks from tree to tree;
Staying up with lighted signs
　Twinkling, "God made me."

Oh, all the little creatures
　Flying, buzzing merrily;
Singing loud from morn 'til night,
　"God made me!"

HOW DO EASTER LILIES HEAR?

My mommy had an Easter plant,
    But the flowers were closed up tight.
I wondered when they would open,
    So I watched it day and night.

I watched it on Good Friday
    And all day Saturday, too.
But the flowers stayed all locked up,
    So I fell asleep—wouldn't you?

But then on Easter morning,
    Right before my sleepy eyes,
There were six white Easter lilies;
    What a beautiful surprise!

Who told them it was Easter
    In the darkness of that room?
I didn't know that lilies could hear
    When God told them to open and bloom.

THE FIVE COBBLERS

Over the hill from Dandelion Sea,
And just two hundred hops
From the bingleberry hedge,
Is a little vale called
Cobblers' Common.
It sits at the foot of
The Mustard Mountains.

Five clever cobblers live there.
Their names, Cobblecut, Stitchtight,
Nailtap, Buffkin and Stampen have
Been passed down for hundreds of
Years in the cobbler family.

Their cobblestone workshop nestles
In the cedar trees, where the path
Begins that leads over
The Mustard Mountains.

Every pair of shoes
The five cobblers make,
Are carefully crafted
For the many travelers
Who go on the long journey
Across the high Mustard Mountains.

Curiously, all the shoes are stamped
According to an old scroll,
Hanging in the workshop, which reads:

"Cobbler family, in this vale,
You are part of a wondrous tale.
In your calling you will find
Shoes to make of every kind,
Since the ones who pass this way
Will need your craft from day to day.
Make each pair with skill—and strong!
Bless them with The Cobbler's Song;
Stamp the Great Seal on every sole,
Thus keep the words of the
    Cobbler's Scroll."

As they were faithful cobblers—
Cobblecut cut…
    Stitchtight stitched…
        Nailtap nailed…
            Buffkin buffed…
And Stampen stamped every
Sole with the Great Seal
Bearing The Cobbler's Song.

Sadly, there was only one line left
Of The Cobbler's Song.
The great seal had gradually worn away
With much use, and all that could be
Read these days were the words,
   "How lovely on the mountains…"

Of course, the great-grandfather cobblers,
Many years ago, had known every
Jot and tittle of The Cobbler's Song.
But word by word
It had slowly faded away.

Nevertheless, the five little cobblers
Faithfully sang the one line left
On The Great Seal,
"How lovely on the mountains…"
Over every pair of shoes they made
To go over the Mustard Mountains.

They were happy to work hard
Making shoes, year after year;
All shapes and sizes,
For all kinds of travelers
Who gladly came to their
Cobblestone workshop.

Some came for two shoes,
  A few inches long;
Some came for four shoes
  To last a life long.
Some came for sandals
  Made from the best leather;
Some came for boots that would
  Stand the worst weather.
Some wanted low shoes,
  And some wanted high.
Some wanted buckles,
  And some, a lace tie.
Some wanted black shoes,
  And some wanted red.
Some wanted brown shoes,
  And some, green instead…

But they *all* wanted to walk over the Mustard Mountains!

One day Stampen said,

"Why do the travelers
    Continue to climb
Up the Mustard Mountains,
    Time after time?
What is their purpose?
    What do they do?
And what is our part
    In making each shoe?
Let's make 'travelers shoes'
    For ourselves, and find out
What The Cobbler's Song
    Is all about."

"I'll gladly cut shoes for that
    Very purpose," said Cobblecut...
"I'll gladly stitch shoes for that
    Very purpose," said Stitchtight...
"I'll gladly nail shoes for that
    Very purpose," said Nailtap...
"I'll gladly buff shoes for that
    Very purpose," said Buffkin...
"And I'll gladly stamp the Great Seal
    On the shoes that will take us over
    The Mustard Mountains," said Stampen.
And they all shook hands on their promise.

137

With cheerful hurry-scurry,
  The cobbling fast began,
As the little cobblers cobbled
  Handsome shoes, to perfect plan.

Cobblecut's were tinted blue;
  Stitchtight's brown with stringing;
Nailtap's green, and Buffkin's gold,
  And Stampen's red, with fringing.

When Stampen stamped the new shoes,
  They sang The Cobbler's Song,
"How lovely on the mountains…"
  Seven times, to make it long.

Bright, early in the morning,
  They marched off up the glen,
Singing in their special shoes;
  Determined little men.

Up, up the rocky pathway,
  And past the waterfall;
Through clumps of swaying bluebells,
  And through the pine trees tall.

Far up the Mustard Mountains,
  And marching at their best,
Five weary little cobblers said,
  "It's time to stop and rest."

138

And there, just off the pathway,
  A small rock shelter stood.
"Welcome Travelers, Rest and Dine,"
  Said a sign made out of wood.

Water bubbled from a spring,
  With mugs in good supply;
And bread and cheese in baskets
  On a polished stump nearby.

All five cobblers bowed their heads,
  To thank God for this care;
And as they ate the good food,
  They heard singing in the air…

"How lovely on the mountains
  Are the Good News feet,
Bringing happy tidings
  Of peace to all they meet…"

"The Cobbler's Song," they whispered,
  "How wondrous are those words.
Where is the music coming from?
  The trees?—the wind?—the birds?"

So once again they set out,
  Then stopped in great surprise,
For as they passed the Whistling Caves,
  A whistling song did arise!

"How lovely on the mountains
　　Are the Good News feet,
Bringing happy tidings
　　Of peace to all they meet.
Feet so quick to climb
　　With the Good, Good News,
Helped along by cobblers
　　Who make the Good News shoes...

"That's more of The Cobbler's Song,"
　　Five voices whispered low,
Peering down the craggy caves
　　Where the song disappeared below.

With staffs in hand, the cobblers
　　Trudged up Cathedral Heights;
"The top!" they cried. "We've reached it!
　　Then gasped at the dazzling sight.

A sunny world lay dancing
　　Over miles of gold and green;
Flowers tinkling, breezes singing
　　With voices of choirs, unseen.

A host of waving banners
　　Flew from cottage roofs around.
Good News rang out everywhere;
　　The peaks were alive with sound!

The cobblers' hearts all jumped for joy
　　At the singing, happy sight;
And best of all, The Cobbler's Song
　　They heard—with power and might!

140

They listened well, and learned it,
As seeking cobblers ought,
And praised God for the Good News
The faithful travelers had brought.

"Let's hurry to the workshop,"
Each cobbler soon agreed,
"And carve back in the Great Seal
The *whole* song for all to read."

Quickly they ran, descending
The path to their little vale;
Knowing now their happy part
In the old scroll's "wondrous tale."

So if you pass their workshop
On the day they're making shoes,
You can hear The Cobbler's Song,
And learn the GOOD, GOOD NEWS from…
Cobblecut, Stitchtight, Nailtap
Buffkin and Stampen…
"How lovely on the mountains
Are the Good News feet,
Bringing happy tidings
Of peace to all they meet.
Feet so quick to climb
With the Good, Good News,
Helped along by cobblers
Who make the Good News shoes;
Publishing salvation
Across the mountain chains,
Feet are bringing Good News!…
OUR GOD REIGNS!"

141

A LITTLE BEE
SAT ON A WALL

A little bee sat on a wall.
"Buzz," said he,
And that was all.
But then I listened carefully
He "Buzzed" again,
And said to me,
"God loves you, little one."

A little bird sat on a twig.
"Chirp," said he,
(Not very big).
But then I listened carefully,
He "Chirped" again,
And said to me,
"God loves you, little one."

142

A little frog sat on a stone.
"Croak," said he,
Just once—alone.
But then I listened carefully,
He "Croaked " again,
And said to me,
"God loves you, little one."

A little owl sat in an oak.
"Whoo," said he,
That's all he spoke.
But then I listened carefully,
He "Whoo-ed " again,
And said to me,
"God loves you, little one."

143

WHERE ARE YOU GOING TO, MY PRETTY MAID?

"Where are you going to,
  My pretty maid?"
"I'm going a-listening,
  Sir," she said.

"May I go with you,
  My pretty maid?"
"You're kindly welcome,
  Sir," she said.

"What will we listen to,
  My pretty maid?"
"My Father's good Words,
  Kind sir," she said.

"Where will we listen,
  My pretty maid?"
"Within Father's house,
  Kind sir," she said.

144

"How will we listen,
  My pretty maid?"
"With all of our heart,
  Kind sir," she said.

"Who is your Father,
  My pretty maid?"
"The Lord God in Heaven,
  Kind sir," she said.

"How can we reach Him,
  My pretty maid?"
"I'll show you the Way,
  Kind sir," she said.

"Jesus, The Way, The Truth
  And The Life,
Will lead you to Him,
  Kind sir," she said.

FROM WIBBLETON TO WOBBLETON

From Wibbleton to Wobbleton,
  A bridge lies in between;
From Wobbleton to Wibbleton,
  The same bridge can be seen.

From Wibbleton to Wobbleton
  Folk start their journey singing;
From Wibbleton to Wobbleton,
  Across the bridge a-ringing!

From Wobbleton to Wibbleton,
  Folk start their journey cringing;
From Wobbleton to Wibbleton,
  Across the bridge a-clinging.

146

From Wibbleton to Wobbleton,
  They cross the bridge robust;
From Wibbleton to Wobbleton,
  Across the bridge in trust!

From Wobbleton to Wibbleton,
  They tremble to start out;
From Wobbleton to Wibbleton,
  Across the bridge in doubt.

From Wibbleton to Wobbleton,
  They very soon get there;
From Wibbleton to Wobbleton,
  Across the bridge in prayer!

From Wobbleton to Wibbleton,
  They cannot stride or hurry;
From Wobbleton to Wibbleton,
  Across the bridge in worry.

From Wibbleton to Wobbleton,
  The bridge is safe and sound;
From Wobbleton to Wibbleton,
  The same bridge can be found!

So, would you live in Wibbleton?
  Or would you live in Wobbleton?
The bridge will give the answer
  When you cross some day.

147

YOU MADE THE MONTHS
FOR ME

JANUARY brings the snow,
  Makes our feet
And fingers glow;
  Gentle Jesus,
Then I know,
  You made the snow for me.

FEBRUARY brings the rain,
  Thaws the frozen
Lakes again;
  Gentle Jesus,
It is plain,
  You made the rain for me.

MARCH brings breezes,
  Loud and shrill,
Stirs the dancing daffodil;
  Gentle Jesus,
All to please,
  You made the breeze for me.

APRIL brings the primrose sweet,
   Scatters daisies
At our feet;
   Gentle Jesus,
Speak the hours,
   You made the flowers for me.

MAY brings flocks of pretty lambs,
   Skipping by
Their fleecy dams;
   Gentle Jesus,
Then I see,
   You made the lambs for me.

JUNE brings perfumed,
   Velvet roses,
Fills the children's
   Hands with posies;
Gentle Jesus,
   My heart knows,
You made the rose for me.

149

Hot JULY brings
  Cooling showers,
Apricots and gillyflowers;
  Gentle Jesus,
By your powers,
  You made the showers for me.

AUGUST brings the sheaves of corn,
  Then the harvest
Home is borne,
  Gentle Jesus,
I believe,
  You made the sheaves for me.

Warm SEPTEMBER brings the fruit,
  Festivals with
Harp and flute;
  Gentle Jesus,
I salute,
  You made the fruit for me.

150

Fresh OCTOBER brings the pheasant,
  Then to gather nuts
Is pleasant;
  Gentle Jesus,
Always present,
  You made the pheasant for me.

Gray NOVEMBER brings bare trees,
  Crackling leaves
Up to our knees;
  Gentle Jesus,
I perceive,
  You made the leaves for me.

Chill DECEMBER brings us home,
  Blazing fire
At evening's gloam;
  Gentle Jesus,
Though I roam,
  You made the home for me.

THE CHIMNEY SWEEP FLIGHT

Cousin Moles were off again
    To Polly-Woggle Park,
When over Chipmunk Chigger
    They saw something rather dark.

It kept growing in the sky,
    Puffing blacker—puffing bigger;
Noggin Mole cried, "Chimneys must be
    Blocked in Chipmunk Chigger!"

"I'm *sure* they're blocked," said Mogie,
    And Tilly nodded, too;
Tolly, Rimpy, Dolly,
    All agreed that was *their* view.

Toggle Mole, excitedly,
    Said, "Send out the alarm!
Send S.O.S. for chimney sweeps,
    Before that cloud does harm!"

Then Noggin got excited,
    "We're turning round," he cried;
"We'll all be heroes!" Toggle cheered,
    "The honors we'll divide."

"S.O.S," they shouted,
    Racing past each house and tree,
And caught the quick attention
    Of Benjamin Bumblebee.

152

Benjamin flew down swiftly,
　　Buzzing over Noggin's head,
"What's all the shouting for?
　　And the S.O.S.?" he said.

"We're rushing back to town,
　　To get help for Chipmunk Chigger,
Their chimney flues are blocked,
　　And the smoke-cloud's getting bigger!"

"Action! We need action!"
　　Seven Cousin Moles cried out.
"I'll fly ahead," said Benjamin,
　　"And warn the town, throughout."

"Hear ye, hear ye, hear ye!"
　　Benjamin Bumblebee buzzed loud,
And soon in Dandelion Sea,
　　He drew a startled crowd.

"Cousin Moles have seen a cloud,
　　As black, as black as night;
Shutting all the sunshine out
　　From Chipmunk Chiggerites."

Grandpa Mole and Brother Rabbit
　　Both came hurrying in,
Along with Charlie Cricket,
　　Who all questioned Benjamin.

"Cousin Moles alerted me,
　　That black cloud's like a cloak;
Through chimney flues that must be cleaned,
　　To conquer all that smoke."

Grandpa Mole spoke to the crowd,
    With words right from his heart,
"Today's the Feast, but there's a job
    To do! Who'll make a start?"

"I will! I'll help! I'm coming!"
    Cried one, and then a dozen.
"We're coming, too!" And with those words,
    Arrived the Moles—each Cousin.

"Come with me, young Cousin Moles,
    You'll find great satisfaction,
In watching Dandelion Sea
    Go quickly into action!"

"Oh, Grandpa Mole, we're ready
    To fly off in your balloon!"
Cousin Moles jumped round and squeaked,
    "We're a chimney sweep platoon!"

With brushes, brooms and buckets,
    Feather dusters, rakes and mops,
A clean-up squad soon rallied round,
    With multi-clean-up props.

"All hands on deck for rescue!"
    Came Brother Rabbit's voice;
"Though we may miss the Feast Day,
    We'll work and *still* rejoice!"

"It's written, whatsoever
    That we do, we do with might;
Take off with prayer and purpose,
    To remove that black-cloud blight."

Charlie launched the *Sharing Ship*,
    All loaded down, and tooting;
With little rafts behind him,
    To the rescue, all commuting.

154

Dressed in chimney sweep tall hats,
    With brushes standing by,
Grandpa Mole and Cousin Moles
    Flew on across the sky.

And there it was before them!
    A quivering, black-blob sight;
Noggin said, "See, Grandpa Mole?
    We all were right! Were right!"

"I'm going to drop," cried Grandpa Mole,
    "Hold on, mole girls and boys!"
But suddenly the cloud broke up,
    With humming, buzzing noise!

It broke in tiny pieces,
    And, what's more, the black cloud spoke!
"Greetings! Greetings! mole balloon,"
    Without a trace of smoke!

155

"Buzzing bees; they're buzzing bees!"
    Cried Cousin Moles, all red.
"Not 'buzzing bees,' we're 'Blessing Bees,' "
    The Queen Bee brightly said.

"We heard that Chipmunk Chigger
    Had no honey for each home.
We're here to bless this little town
    With plans of honeycomb."

Grandpa Mole then spoke right up,
    "Indeed, I'm quite relieved,
To find that Chipmunk Chigger's
    Not smoked out, as we believed."

"Goodbye, good moles. Goodbye, balloon.
    We must be off and working."
The bees flew off, but Cousin Moles
    Crouched in the basket, lurking.

Grandpa Mole laughed as he turned
    The big balloon around,
"You might as well stand up," said he,
    "And tell our friends on ground."

"Tell them what the black cloud was?"
  The Cousin Moles all mumbled.
"Of course, and they will all be glad
  Our Feast Day hasn't crumbled."

    "The Feast! The Feast! We'll be on time!
      Everyone still can go,"
    Happily shouted seven moles;
      "Good News! to all below."

      "Turn back, turn back, it's false alarm!
        No danger, in the least;
      We're still all clean; we're still on time,
        To celebrate the Feast!"

The *Sharing Ship* and all the rafts,
  "Toot-tooted," merrily,
As mops and pails turned homeward sails
  To Dandelion Sea.

When Cousin Moles had landed home,
  (No longer chimney-hatters)
Grandpa Mole said, "Little tongues
  Can kindle such great matters."

"We've learned our lesson, Grandpa Mole,
  'Be *sure* before you tell!'"
They blew a kiss, and Grandpa smiled,
  "All's well that ends so well."

157

I THINK GOD LIKES EVERY KIND OF SONG

I think God likes
  Every kind of song:
Every-kind-of-praise song,
  Old-or-nowadays song;
Kneeling-down-devout songs,
  Stomp-along-and-shout songs;
Hushy-quiet-soft-songs,
  Hats-all-on-or-off songs;
Sing-with-all-your-might songs,
  Dainty-sound-polite songs;
Whispered-little-prayer songs,
  Rocking-in-the-chair songs;
I think God likes
  Every kind of praise.

158

I think God likes
  Every kind of praise:
Hurry-fast-along-songs,
  Take-a-long-time-long songs;
Leave-the-third-verse-out songs,
  Can't-sing-it-without songs;
Barely-can-be-heard songs,
  All-alone-or-shared songs;
Big-cathedral-choir songs,
  Sitting-by-the-fire songs;
Little-bits-of-snatch songs,
  Concerts-by-the-batch songs;
I think God likes
  Every kind of song!

159

IS ANYBODY LISTENING?

Is anybody listening,
Listening, listening?
Is anybody listening,
Listening to me?
I saw a mouse
Stand on his head!
I saw a butterfly—
All red!
I ran home fast to tell
All that there was to see.

But no one even stopped and said,
"You saw a *mouse*
Stand on his head!
You saw a *butterfly*—
All red!
What marvelous things
You just have said!"
Instead, I just went up to bed,
And told it all to me!
Is anybody listening,
Listening, listening?
Is anybody listening,
Listening to me?

160

I disappeared
Inside my bed;
All you could see
Was just my head;
I closed my ears so tight
No sound could reach in me.

But though I shut the sound all out,
A little voice
Began to sprout
Inside myself,
And rose about
With words, just like
A waterspout
That swished and swirled
All round about,
As plain, as plain could be:
"Is anybody listening?
Listening, listening?
Is anybody listening,
Listening to ME?"

"*I* saw the mouse
Stand on his head;
I saw the butterfly—
All red!
I saw you run to tell
All that there was to see.
And when you hid inside your bed,
I whispered in your ear and said,
'Let all the little children
Come and talk to ME!'
For I am *always* listening,
Listening, listening;
I am *always* listening,
Listening carefully."

161

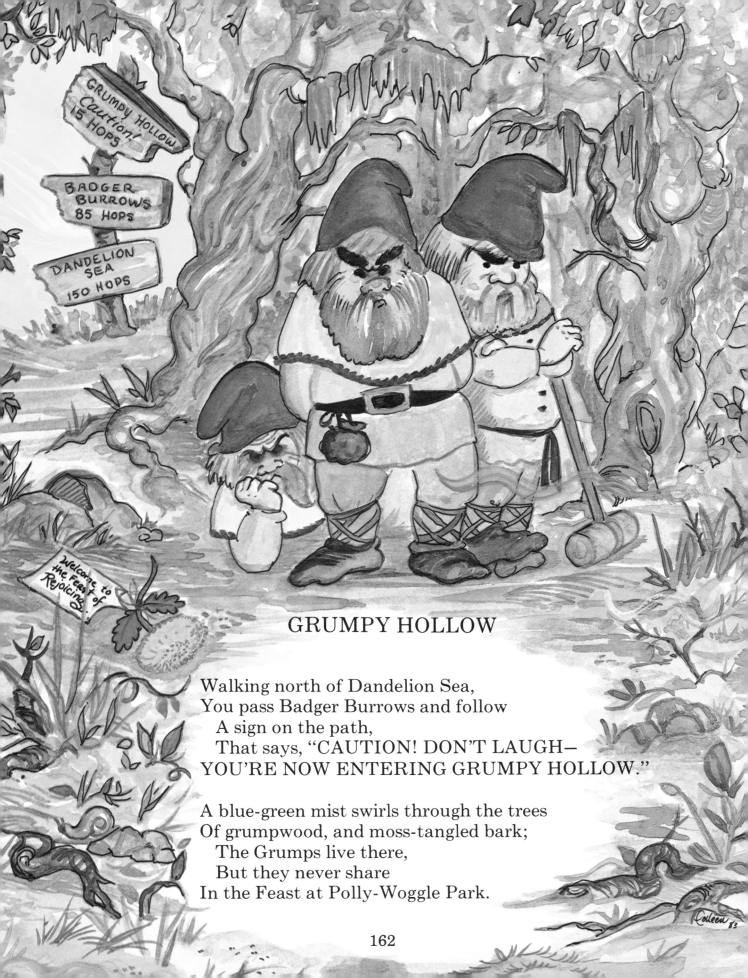

GRUMPY HOLLOW

Walking north of Dandelion Sea,
You pass Badger Burrows and follow
  A sign on the path,
    That says, "CAUTION! DON'T LAUGH—
YOU'RE NOW ENTERING GRUMPY HOLLOW."

A blue-green mist swirls through the trees
Of grumpwood, and moss-tangled bark;
  The Grumps live there,
    But they never share
In the Feast at Polly-Woggle Park.

They never come out to make new friends
With the rest of the countryside;
    They don't like the sun,
    Or words such as "fun,"
Their vocabulary's not very wide.

It mainly consists of words like, "grump,"
"Crabapple," and "bitter," or "sour."
    "Gloomy" and "glum,"
    "Complain" and "humdrum,"
They practice these words by the hour.

At last here's the day all have waited for,
And the Grumps are gathering together;
    Dr. Frump is the Chief,
    And grumps through his teeth,
"No doubt, we'll have gloomy-glum weather."

"Now, Grumps, as you know, today is the Feast,
The Feast of Grumbling, no less;
    As your usual host,
    I suggest make the most
Of your worries and general distress."

"We'll start with our song, then follow along
With a game of croquet, as we do;
    The song has no key,
    But try following me,
You can struggle, the pitch to pursue."

        "And now…
        Let the Feast of Grumbling begin…"

        *"Some folks say
        Things are looking up,
        We say things
        Are always looking down.
        Things get worse,
        Worse from head to toe;
        Be prepared for melancholy woe,*

        *Grump, grump, grump,
        Grump, grump, grump,
        It's our trade
        To grump, grump, grump.*

        *We can frown,
        The biggest frowns in town,
        We can make
        The grumpiest of sounds;
        We can argue
        Every pro and con,
        We can feel
        The worst of anyone.*

        *Grump, grump, grump,
        Grump, grump, grump,
        It's our trade
        To grump, grump, grump."*

"Well sung," said Dr. Frump,
"And now...Let the game begin..."

In blue-green tunics, with blue-green mallets,
The Grumps shuffled into position,
  Scuffling and mumbling,
  Gruffling and grumbling,
According to long-time tradition.

"Now, struggle to play together this day,
But not *too* close, mind you," Frump called.
  Then with the first blow,
  A Grump cried, "My toe!
Ouch! Ouch! you hit *me*, not the ball!"

"You got in the way," his partner replied,
"You should have known better, instead."
  "Don't say that word, 'better,'
  My mind it will fetter,
Get Dr. Frump, quick, my toe's red!"

"Glum-double, double, toil and trouble,
Take two sour grapes in a hurry,"
  Said Dr. Frump
  To the injured Grump,
"You're sure to get worse, so don't worry."

165

Colleen M. Scott

Then Frump tipped his head at a sound he heard,
Like the trill of a lilting swallow,
   "What an awful noise,
   It spoils my poise,
Someone singing in Grumpy Hollow?"

Brighter and clearer the singing came,
With happy songs praising and voicing,
   'Twas Smiley Saroo,
   With his oil bottles, too,
On his way to the Feast of Rejoicing!

Dr. Frump frowned his most scowly-frown,
And peered through the thick grumpwood tangle:
   "This is hallowed ground
   For grumping sound,
Not for singing such jingle-jangle!"

166

"Who are you? You don't belong here,
We don't need your smiles and your song,"
　　Dr. Frump scowled,
　　Right down to his jowl,
"You've taken a path that is wrong!"

"I am the Smiley Saroo, good friends,
And this is the right kind of place,
　　For a Smiley Saroo
　　With what's good for you,"
Said Saroo with a twinkling face.

"That face hurts my eyes, that voice hurts my ears,"
Said one Grump right after another.
　　"You need a good dose
　　Of crabapple juice,
To stop all your jovial bother."

"What do you do with your dreadful self,
And your singing that makes my ears thump?
　　It's a serious thing,
　　To make the ears ring
Of the Chief of the Grumps—Dr. Frump."

"Well, Dr. Frump, it's a pleasure to tell
Of my calling, and just what I do.
　　And now that you ask,
　　It's a happy task
Living life as a Smiley Saroo."

And before the Grumps could grump again,
The Smiley Saroo twirled his cane;
  With laughter and dance,
  A skip and a prance,
In his song he began to explain:

*"When I see folks in any town
Start to grumble, and start to frown,
This funny bird, called "Smiley Saroo,"
Pulls up their lips, and they smile, too.
Now a Smiley Saroo
Has a smile you can catch,
And wherever he goes
People smile by the batch..."*

"Stop! Stop! Don't finish!"
  Cried all the Grumps...

"You'll not catch us smiling down here, Saroo,"
Said Frump. "And you're wasting our time;
  Your alien heart,
  Oil bottles and cart,
Are spoiling our Festival's clime."

He called to the Grumps, "Let's sing our own song,
March on!" And they circled the Hollow;
  With notes woebegone,
  The Grumps fumbled on,
Intent in their grumping to wallow.

Plodding around, not one saw the sign
That hung on the front of the cart,
  "Merry hearts do good,
  Like a medicine should,
Oil of Gladness will bring a new heart!"

OIL OF GLADNESS

*Merry Hearts Do Good
Like a Medicine Should.
Oil of Gladness will
Bring a New Heart!"*

Then Smiley Saroo took some of his oil,
And when the Grumps came to a halt,
   With twinkling eyes,
   He said, "I'll advise
My medicine oil for your fault."

"Here, Dr. Frump, is a remedy you need,
This is just the right medicine for you."
   "Medicine, you say?
   Don't hurry away,
You're now talking our language, Saroo."

"It's a bitter, horrible-tasting stuff,
And of course, no results," Frump said.
   "Well, this kind of oil
   You don't drink at all;
I'll just pour it all over your head!"

"Feels good to look down, Saroo, feels good,"
Agreed Dr. Frump, bending down,
   As out of the spout
   Oil of Gladness poured out
All over his grumpy crown.

"Come on Grumps, in your favorite position,
Bend down, everyone, here by me;
   Hats off, to a man,
   Let's get all that we can
Of this medicine, while it is free."

169

So the Oil of Gladness trickled on down
All the Grumps there in Grumpy Hollow,
   Working its power,
   In joyful shower,
With Saroo knowing all that would follow.

Lightly, then bubbling, and bursting aloud,
The merriment grew and grew;
   With laughter and shouts,
   And dancing about,
All the Grumps skipped round Smiley Saroo!

"A merry heart is good for your health,"
Said Saroo, "and is good for your face;
   A cheerful mind
   Will work wonders, you'll find,
In a wisdom that's not commonplace."

"Today is the Feast of Rejoicing,
Why not join me and all come along."
   "We're no longer Grumps,"
   Replied Dr. Frump,
"And we'll join you right *now* in a song!"

Happily singing, they blew the green mist
Away, and the Hollow turned bright;
   And in perfect key,
   This song, merrily,
Brought in rainbows of golden sunlight:

"If you think a merry heart
   Is good for your health,
All in favor say, 'Aye!'
   If you think God's blessing
Is the greatest of wealth,
   All in favor say, 'Aye!'
If you think a drop of Oil
   Of Gladness will raise
Happy hands of clapping
   That will brighten your days,
If you think that you can sing
   A new song of praise,
   All in favor say…
   All in favor say…
   All in favor say, 'AYE!'"

And the happy Grumps cheered
And said…"AYE! AYE! AYE!"

171

THREE LITTLE KITTENS

Three little kittens
   Lost their mittens,
And they began to cry,
   "Oh, mother dear,
   We sadly fear
We lost our mittens nearby."

"Lost your mittens!
   Then little kittens,
Take lamps and look, don't cry.
   Sweep every nook,
   And seek and look
For mittens, both low and high."

Three little kittens
   Found their mittens,
And joyfully did cry,
   "Oh, mother dear,
   See here, see here!
Our mittens we found close by!"

"Found your mittens!
   Good little kittens,
Bring all your friends for pie.
   The lost is found!
   We'll dance around!
Three little kittens and I."

LITTLE FISHY
IN THE BROOK

Little fishy in the brook,
  I can catch you quickly, look!
Bigger fishy in the lake,
  Needs more work for me to take.
Biggest fish down in the sea,
  Catching you takes two of me!
Great, strong fish down in the deep,
  Takes twelve boys to catch and keep!

173

DOWN A GRASSY BANK

Down a grassy bank
In the bright warm sun,
Lives a wise mother mouse
And her little mouse—
         ONE!
"LOVE," said the mother,
"I love," said the one;
So they lived in love
In the bright warm sun.

Down a grassy bank
Where the stream runs through,
Lives a wise mother fish
And her little fishes—
                    TWO!
"JOY!" said the mother,
"We've joy," said the two;
So they lived in joy
Where the stream runs through.

175

Down a grassy bank
In a willow tree,
Lives a wise mother dove
And her little doves—
        THREE!
"PEACE," said the mother,
"We've peace," said the three;
So they lived in peace
In the willow tree.

Down a grassy bank
Near the beavers' shore,
Lives a wise mother beaver
And her little beavers—
        FOUR!
"PATIENCE," said the mother,
"We've patience," said the four;
So they gnawed in patience
Near the beavers' shore.

Down a grassy bank
Where the otters dive,
Lives a wise mother otter
And her little otters—
        FIVE!
"KINDNESS," said the mother,
"We've kindness," said the five;
So they played in kindness
Where the otters dive.

Down a grassy bank
Where the acorns mix,
Lives a wise mother squirrel
And her little squirrels—
        SIX!
"GOODNESS," said the mother,
"We've goodness," said the six;
So they shared in goodness
Where the acorns mix.

Down a grassy bank
Looking up to Heaven,
Lives a wise mother frog
And her little frogs—
      SEVEN!
"FAITH!" said the mother,
"We've faith," said the seven;
So they jumped in faith
Looking up to Heaven.

Down a grassy bank
Where the ducklings skate,
Lives a wise mother duck
And her little ducklings—
      EIGHT!
"GENTLE," said the mother,
"We're gentle," said the eight;
So they were most gentle
Where the ducklings skate.

Down a grassy bank
Where the rabbits dine,
Lives a wise mother rabbit
And her little rabbits—
NINE!
"CONTROL!" said the mother,
"We've control," said the nine;
So they nibbled in control
Where the rabbits dine.

COCK ROBIN GOT UP EARLY

Cock Robin got up early,
  On baby's first birthday,
And flew to baby's house
  To sing a happy roundelay:
"Precious little baby,
  Jesus loves you dear;
Grow to be more like Him,
  As I return each year."

KNOCK AT THE DOOR

Knock at the door,
Peep in.
Lift up the latch,
Walk in!
Welcome, dear Lord!
Join in.
Lift up our hands,
Praise Him!

THERE WAS AN OLD WOMAN
LIVED UNDER A HILL

There was an old woman
   Lived under a hill.
She was an old woman
   Of very good will.

Baked apples she gave
   To children who came
To learn about Jesus,
   And call on His Name.

Great stories she told
   Of Samson and Paul,
And prophets of old
   Who answered God's call.

The children all loved her,
   For she was the one
Who told how God loved them,
   And sent His dear Son.

LITTLE POLLY FLINDERS

Little Polly Flinders,
  Knows a word that hinders;
Instead of "might,"
  She says, "Must, must, must!"
Another word is "doubt,"
  Which she just turns roundabout,
And cheerily says,
  "I will trust, trust, trust!"

SOMEBODY!

A little knock came quietly.
They said, "Don't look,
It's *nobody*."
But I thought it was
Somebody!
And so I looked,
Because, you see,
God did not make a
Nobody!
He makes a special
Somebody!
He makes a special
You and *me!*
And so I looked,
I looked, you see,
To see that special
Somebody!

I FILLED A LITTLE BASKET

I filled a little basket
  With some cherries from a tree;
I filled a little box
  With some shells along the sea;
I filled a little bag
  With some speckled rocks I found;
I filled a little hole
  With some soil piled on the ground;

I filled my little mouth
  With some happy songs to God;
I filled my little hands
  With His kindly Shepherd's rod;
I filled my little ears
  With His Words, to guide my feet;
Then *He* filled little *me*,
  With His love and Spirit, sweet.

THIS IS THE WAY

This is the way the fathers ride,
  "Emmanuel! Praise the Lord!"

This is the way the mothers ride,
  "Bread of Life! Praise the Lord!"

This is the way the children ride,
  "Precious Jesus! Praise the Lord!"

This is the way the grandpas ride,
  "Counsellor! Praise the Lord!"

This is the way the grandmas ride,
  "Comforter! Praise the Lord!"

This is the way the young men ride,
  "Lion of Judah! Praise the Lord!"

This is the way the ladies ride,
  "Rose of Sharon! Praise the Lord!"

This is the way the uncles ride,
  "Prince of Peace! Praise the Lord."

This is the way the aunties ride,
  "Living Word!   Praise the Lord!"

Fathers, mothers, sisters, brothers,
  Know these Names, and many others;
But, returning home, they'll sing,
  "Lord of Lords, and King of Kings!"

184

THE BEST TOUCH OF ALL!

I love to touch my rabbit's nose,
 I love to touch a silky rose;
I love to touch my pony's mane,
 I love to touch a showery rain;
I love to touch my cushion chair,
 I love to touch my teddy bear;
I love to touch my new boots' leather,
 I love to touch my peacock feather;
I love to touch my little sail,
 I love to touch my puppy's tail;
I love to touch my big red ball,
 But there's a touch that's best of all!...

When Mommy and Daddy touch me!

COUSIN MOLES—
THE TIME THIEVES

Tilly, Tolly and Dolly,
　　With Toggle Mole, as well,
Noggin, Mogie and Rimpy Mole,
　　Are hurrying, you can tell.

Seven little Cousin Moles,
　　As chipper as can be,
Are riding off to wake the town
　　Of Dippley Dockerlee.

They want to make the Feast Day
　　Last longer—if they can;
So they got up very early
　　To carry out their plan.

They rode past Grandpa Mole's house,
　　And Polly-Woggle Park,
Through Dandelion Sea's green lanes,
　　To reach the bridge landmark.

Pedalling hard across the bridge,
　　Through fields of four-o'clocks,
At last they came to the village
　　Where everything goes, "Tick-Tock."

186

In Dippley Dockerlee, you see,
   Are flocks and flocks and flocks,
Of roly-poly Docker Bugs
   Who look like little clocks.

The Docker Bugs are careful
   To redeem the time each day;
They work and praise while letting,
   "Yea" be "Yea," and "Nay" be "Nay!"

The clockmaker in the village
   Checks the sundial twice a day;
And four-o'clock flowers open,
   Keeping time in *their* own way.

A music clock in the Tower
   Booms each hour, a mighty "BONG!"
And at eight o'clock each morning
   It plays the town's theme song:

"Docker Bugs, we're Docker Bugs,
Roly-poly Docker Bugs,
As we roly right along,
'Praise The Lord!'
That is our song.
We redeem the time each day,
'Yea' is 'Yea,' and 'Nay' is 'Nay',
But there's always time to say,
'Praise The Lord!'
The Docker Way."

187

Now, Cousin Moles rode into town
   As Docker Bugs still slept;
In summertime they sleep outdoors,
   So Cousin Moles softly crept.

"We're going to turn their clocks back,"
   Toggle Mole said, "so that we
Can make a happy, *longer* day
   For Dippley Dockerlee!"

So, one by one, they turned back
   All the clocks, from six to four;
And changed the Tower clock
   Between the "Tick-Tock" of each snore.

Then Cousin Moles departed,
   And left the town in bed,
Not knowing they were being watched
   From high up overhead!

For Grandpa Mole and Mother Goose
   Had watched the whole affair,
While dropping invitations
   To the Feast, from in mid-air.

"Now, what are Cousin Moles up to?"
   Grandpa Mole asked curiously;
"I think since all our work is done,
   I'll drop you off and see."

At Mother Goose's cottage,
   Grandpa Mole came gently down,
"Your own front door, dear Mother Goose,
   As soft as eider-down!"

"I'll meet you later at the Feast;
   I'm bringing two young friends,"
Mother Goose said. "Off you go!
   To help Moles make amends."

Now...Docker Bugs get up at six,
    And start the day with song;
But they had overslept two hours
    When the Tower clock rang "BONG!"

Soon everyone was busy
    In the things that make up days;
Yet in all their busy moments
    They did not forget to Praise!

The old clockmaker on his way
    To open shop at nine,
Picked a bunch of four-o'clocks,
    And checked the sundial's time.

The sundial's shadow pointed to
    Almost eleven o'clock;
"How can that be? Just look at me!"
    He gasped in "tick-tock" shock.

He hurried to the Tower clock;
    Mayor Dippley Dock was there,
Arranging for a big parade
    Around the market square.

"Mayor Dippley Dock, we've lost two hours.
    Someone has stolen time!
The sundial shows eleven o'clock,
    And Docker Bugs show nine!"

190

Three hundred Docker Bugs looked down
  To check clocks, large and small;
And *everyone* read, "nine o'clock,"
  Not sundial time at all.

Mayor Dippley Dock went up the Tower
  And called to his parade,
"Someone has stolen two hours time;
  A 'Time-thief' escapade!"

"They've tampered with our Docker clocks,
  But the one clock they forgot,
Is God's big sun! So Praise the Lord!
  We know their 'Time-thief' plot."

"The hours we've lost call for a change,
  We must cancel our parade;
'Dockers For Soccer' will have to wait,
  It's time for our work and trade."

With disappointed faces,
  And knowing they must hurry,
The Docker Bugs re-set their clocks,
  With fussing, fret and scurry.

Mayor Dippley Dock cried, "Dockers!
  We *redeem* the time each day;
If we react in blame and fault,
  We'll waste *more* time away."

"Our time may have been stolen,
  But good humor we must keep;
Right now, let's all forgive the thieves,
  Then *extra* time we'll reap!"

Meanwhile, to celebrate the Feast,
    Cousin Moles were gathering peas,
When Grandpa Mole walked through the patch
    And said, "Attention, please!"

"A certain situation,
    In Dippley Dockerlee,
Regarding time on Docker clocks,
    May cause an emergency."

"Emergency!" squeaked Cousin Moles,
    With voices in dismay;
"Dear Grandpa Mole, we only meant
    To give them a longer day."

Grandpa Mole leaned forward,
    And Cousin Moles grew red;
"I'm sure the Docker Bugs will all
    Forgive you," Grandpa said.

So Tilly, Tolly, Dolly,
    And Toggle Mole at rear;
With Noggin, Mogie, Rimpy Mole,
    All pedalling in high gear,
Rode back to say, "We're sorry,"
    To Dippley Dockerlee;
Then seven little Cousin Moles
    Came home so happily!

A FAMILY

Who ever could have thought of it?
A little house with room to fit
A Mommy-mom and Daddy-dad,
With boys and girls
To make them glad!
Could *you* have ever thought of it?
I never could, I do admit.
What lovely plans *GOD* must have knit,
For *HE'S* the One who thought of it—
A FAMILY!

MONDAY'S CHILD

Monday's child will seek God's face,
Tuesday's child is full of grace,
Wednesday's child in faith will grow,
Thursday's child God's love will show,
Friday's child is loving and giving,
Saturday's child thanks God for living,
And the child that is born
On the Lord's first day,
Will trust Him as He leads the way.

WHY DON'T BIRDS WEAR COATS IN WINTER?

Why don't birds wear coats in winter?
  Why don't they wear woolly boots?
Why don't they wear hats and mittens,
  Underwear and zippered suits?

All they have is colored feathers,
  Winter, spring and summer, too.
Why don't birds wear coats in winter?
  Oh, I wish, I wish I knew!

Boys like me, we have to dress up
  Warm and cozy from the snow.
How Cock Robin flies about without a coat,
  I do not know.

I will tell you
How the birds can live
Without those clothes.
God warms them
From their tiny feet
Up to their tiny nose.
Some He sends away
For winter,
To the lands
Of sunshine bright;
And those He keeps
At home with you,
He keeps warm
Day and night.

Why don't birds wear coats in winter?
  That little sparrow at my door?
God, who made them, keeps them cozy.
  So I'll not worry anymore.

SIMPLE SIMON

Simple Simon met a Pieman
   Going to the fair.
Said Simple Simon to the Pieman,
   "Can you count your hair?"

Said the Pieman to Simple Simon,
   "No one can count hairs, son."
Said Simple Simon to the Pieman,
   "God counts them, every one!"

Simple Simon went to school
  To ask the master there,
"Can you count all of the stars
  And tell me the number, sir?"

Said the master to Simple Simon,
  "There is no way to count."
Said Simple Simon to the master,
  "God knows the whole amount!"

Simple Simon met a climber
  Climbing peaks, one day.
Said Simple Simon to the climber,
  "What does this mountain weigh ?"

Said the climber to Simple Simon,
  "No one knows that, I'm afraid."
Said Simple Simon to the climber,
  "God weighed it when it was made!"

199

HEY, DIDDLE, DIDDLE

Hey, diddle, diddle,
  Me and my fiddle,
The cat sang along in tune;
  My little dog laughed
Enjoying our song,
  How God hung the stars and the moon!

LITTLE EARTHEN VESSELS

God has put a treasure
    In a little earthen pot.
It's such a precious treasure,
    Clean and pure, without a spot!

Yes! All across the world,
    Where the Name of Jesus sounds,
In little pots that love Him,
    This great treasure can be found,

IN...

Brown pots
And black pots,
And all-in-a-stack pots;
And pots that are fancy and plain;
In red pots
And white pots,
And heavy and light pots;
And yellow pots covered with cane.

In tall pots
And short pots,
And sturdy support-pots,
And tiny pots bobbing around;
In smooth pots
And rough pots,
And tumble-and-scuff pots,
And pots hidden way underground!

In clear pots
And flecked pots,
And close neck-to-neck pots,
And pots with a wee, little spout;
In north pots
And south pots,
And big open-mouth pots,
With handles on some; some without.

So that...

North, west, south and eastwards,
   And in any language, too,
You can ask God for this treasure
   To come in and live in you!

That's why all across the world,
   Boys and girls — and grown-ups, too,
Are the little earthen vessels
   For God's treasure to shine through.

TOM, TOM, THE PIPER'S SON

Tom, Tom, the Piper's son,
  Stole a pig and away did run;
The Lord said,
  "Tom, take it back right away,
Or you'll never be happy,
  Day after day."

THERE WAS A CROOKED MAN

There was a crooked man
  Who walked a crooked mile.
He never could straighten up,
  So never did smile.
He found a little book
  That said, "God makes
The crooked straight!"
  He believed,
And straightened up with smiles
  And jumped the garden gate!

MRS. SPARROW'S
STOLEN EGG

Mrs. Sammy Sparrow
  Had just laid two dotted eggs,
In a nest inside a steeple,
  And off she ran on little legs.

She ran to tell Mrs. Robin,
  "My eggs are marked with an 'E'!
The dots are all arranged that way,
  Would you like to come and see?"

"Yes, I would love to see them,
  What unusual eggs they must be;
But would you take a moment
  For a fresh red raspberry?"

Then while those two dear ladies
    Shared a breakfast raspberry,
Mrs. Blackbird flew on by,
    And those two little eggs did see.

She was quite unhappy,
    Because, that very day,
Her own two eggs had broken
    As she laid them both away.

Now here before her eyes
    Were two eggs, and Mother gone!
"Mrs. Sparrow shouldn't care
    If I steal away just one!"

Then quickly Mrs. Blackbird
   Stole one egg, and off she flew,
Just as Mrs. Sparrow
   And Mrs. Robin came back, too.

"Oh, dear! One egg is missing!"
   Mrs. Sparrow cried loudly.
"Please, Mrs. Robin, watch this egg,
   While I fly to Dandelion Sea."

"Sammy is down there helping
   Grandpa Mole to gather wood;
They won't believe what's happened
   In our happy neighborhood."

She flew to Grandpa Mole's house,
    And her tears they dripped and fell,
As she told her sad, sad story;
    And then Sammy cried as well.

"I think that I can solve this,"
    Grandpa Mole said. "Here's a plan;
As Judge of Dandelion Sea,
    I will judge the best I can."

"You say when you came home,
    Mrs. Blackbird flew away?
Then let us go and talk with her,
    And for wisdom let us pray."

GRANDPA
MOLE

So Sammy walked with Mrs. Sparrow;
  Grandpa Mole wore his judge's hat;
And all three walked together
  To Mrs. Blackbird's for a chat.

"Good-day to you, Mrs. Blackbird."
  "It's not a good day," she replied.
"Today my two eggs were broken,
  And I cried, and cried, and cried.

"What is that you're sitting on?
  It looks like an egg to me,"
Grandpa Mole said slowly;
  "Did you have two eggs or three?"

"Oh, I forgot this dotted one,
  Your pardon I must beg."
But peeping out was the dotted 'E';
  Mrs. Sparrow cried, "That's my egg!"

"No! No! this egg is my egg,
 Mrs. Sparrow; you're quite wrong."
"I'm not! The 'E' that marks that egg
 Tells me where it belongs."

Then Grandpa Mole coughed loudly,
 And said, "Ladies, listen to me.
I will decide this matter,
 As Judge of Dandelion Sea."

"We'll share the egg between you,
 By cutting it in two;
Mrs. Sparrow, you take half;
 Mrs. Blackbird, take half, too."

"Oh, no, please do not cut the egg,
  Let Mrs. Blackbird keep it here,"
Mrs. Sparrow quickly said,
  While swallowing a tear.

"I think we should divide it;
  I don't care if it's cut in two,"
Mrs. Blackbird shouted back;
  'Twas then Grandpa Mole really knew —

The real bird mother cared,
  Because she loved her egg, so dear,
And didn't want it hurt at all —
  So Grandpa Mole spoke loud and clear:

"As Judge of Dandelion Sea,
  I hereby now make this decree:
That Mrs. Sparrow is rightfully
  The mother of this egg marked 'E'."

211

Mrs. Blackbird rushed away
  With ruffled feather-clothes,
But Mrs. Sparrow saw a tear
  Roll down her neighbor's nose.

Mrs. Sparrow's little heart
  Felt sad, and so said she,
"I don't think Mrs. Blackbird
  Meant those things she said to me."

Grandpa Mole took off his hat
  And said, "I do agree,
But how to win your friend back
  Takes a special remedy."

"It is written we should be kind,
  And quick to love one another;
Be tenderhearted and forgive
  When we hurt each other."

"It's the best and only way
  To win a hurting friend;
And here's a good suggestion
  To bring about a happy end:"

"There are two orphaned sparrows
  Who need a home and care;
And Mrs. Blackbird's house and heart
  Need someone, too, to share."

"Grandpa Mole, how wise you are!
  Let's go there right away,
To tell our friend, Mrs. Blackbird,
  This is going to be a GOOD DAY!"

LONDON BRIDGE IS FALLING DOWN

London Bridge is falling down,
  Falling down, falling down,
London Bridge is falling down,
  My fair lady.

Build it up with wood and clay,
  Wood and clay, wood and clay,
Build it up with wood and clay,
  My fair lady.

Wood and clay will wash away,
  Wash away, wash away,
Wood and clay will wash away,
  My fair lady.

Build it up with iron and steel,
  Iron and steel, iron and steel,
Build it up with iron and steel,
  My fair lady.

Iron and steel will bend and bow,
  Bend and bow, bend and bow,
Iron and steel will bend and bow,
  My fair lady.

Build it up with silver and gold,
Silver and gold, silver and gold,
Build it up with silver and gold,
My fair lady.

Silver and gold will steal away,
Steal away, steal away,
Silver and gold will steal away,
My fair lady.

What will build up London Bridge,
  London Bridge, London Bridge?
What will build up London Bridge?
  My fair lady.

Only God's Chief Cornerstone,
  Cornerstone, Cornerstone,
Only God's Chief Cornerstone,
  My fair lady.

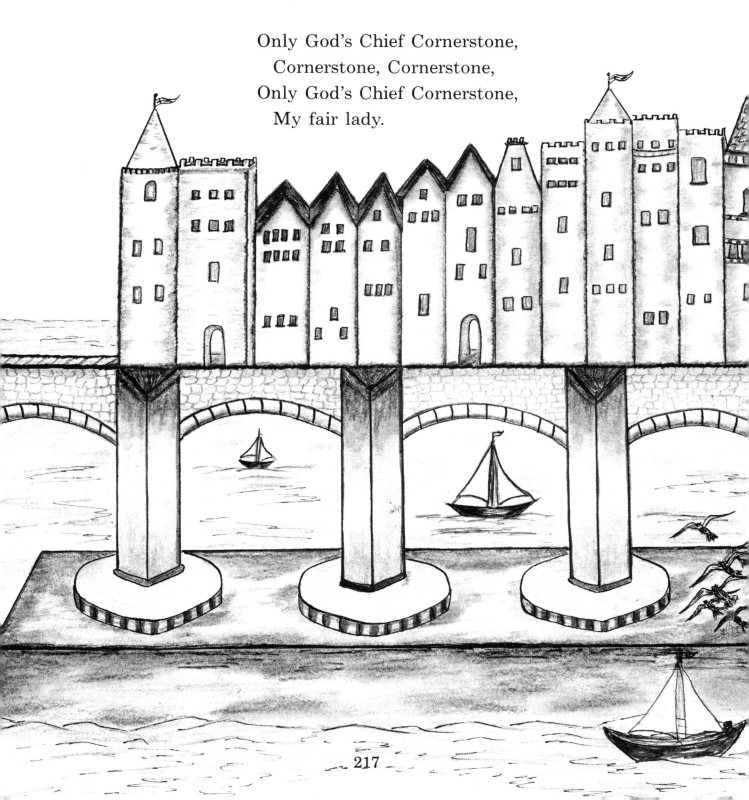

IF TURNIP SEEDS GROW TURNIPS

If turnip seeds grow turnips,
    And greens grow spinach greens;
If carrot seeds grow carrots,
    And bean seeds bring up beans;
If lettuce seeds grow lettuce,
    And Brussel seeds grow sprouts;
If pea seeds always bring up peas —
    Then what goes in comes out!

So kind words bring up kindness,
    And bad words will grow sadness;
Forgiving words will grow forgiveness,
    Glad words will grow gladness!
So watch the little seeds you plant,
    In all you say and do;
For what you sow is what you reap!
    Be proud of what you grew!

WHAT'S THE NEWS
OF THE DAY?

What's the news of the day
    Good neighbor, I pray?
They say the King soon
    Will outshine the moon!

SOLOMON GRUNDY

Solomon Grundy said one Sunday,
  "I think that I can make a Monday.
I will improve the present day
    And add two extra hours for play."

"Not only that, the sun will shine
    From four-o'clock to half-past nine.
I'll make it rain at my command,
    On chosen ones across the land."

So Solomon woke at half-past three,
    Ran up the hill and climbed a tree.
And as the time was nearing four,
    Solomon Grundy gave a roar!

"Come up, *now*, sun! Begin my day!
   Come two hours early for extra play."
But no light came — to his surprise!
   Shout as he would, the sun didn't rise!

"The sun can't hear me; it's out of sight;
   Those extra hours I'll make tonight."
Then as he jumped down from the tree,
   An owl that watched on said, "That can't be!"

"The sunrise and sunset you can't persuade,
   For this is the day the Lord hath made."
But Solomon Grundy, haughtily,
   Said, "This is the day named after me!"

"It's Grunday today, I'll make it rain
  Down on the fields of Farmer Slade's grain.
He is deserving; honest and fair;
  I'll tell a big cloud to rain over there."

He looked all around, no cloud was in sight.
  "I'll push one together with all my might.
There must be a way to make clouds," said he,
  Then a fawn that watched on said, "That can't be!"

"God gives the rain for *all*, not just Slade,
  For this is the day the Lord hath made!"
But Solomon Grundy, haughtily,
  Said, "This is the day named after me!"

Solomon sighed, "My day I can't waste,
  Those two extra hours I must find in haste.
It's now two-o'clock! I'll jump on this stack,
  And insist the sun go two hours back!"

"Sun, *please* go back at the hour's chime!"
  But the sun stayed in place in perfect time.
"There must be a way to make time," said he;
  Then a dove that watched on said, "That can't be!"

"God has fixed time, you cannot evade,
  For this is the day the Lord hath made!"
But Solomon Grundy, wearily,
  Said, "This day I tried to name after me!"

223

"But I can't make a day, I can't make it rain,
    I can't guide the sun, it's hard to explain.
I can't find the time or master-key,
    To make up a day named after me."

So Solomon Grundy began to see
    That GOD makes the days, and so said he,
"I'll stop this foolish, day-making crusade,
    And rejoice in the day the LORD hath made!"

BENJAMIN BUMBLEBEE
AND THE GIANT TUMBLEWEED

Nestled in a sunflower
    In Dandelion Sea,
Reading his daily lesson,
    Was Benjamin Bumblebee.

The sunflower began to sway,
    As a breeze began to blow;
But Benjamin kept on reading,
    And rocking to and fro.

"If I say this verse ten times,
    Then perhaps I'll come to see
What these words can really mean
    To a learning bumblebee!"

"All things work together for good
    To those who love the Lord;
All things work together for good
    To those who love the Lord."

"All things work together for good—
  Now, is that three times or four?
All things work together…" "SWOOSH",
  In rushed a wind with a roar!

It blew the roofs off houses,
  And lifted a hive of bees;
Then took Charlie Cricket's mail bag
  Sailing over the trees!

ZOOM! went Grandpa Mole's balloon;
  SWISH! went thousands of seeds!
And then that mighty wind swept up
  A giant tumbleweed!

It raced this way and that way,
  And went bouncing everywhere;
Then bumped the flower with Benjamin
  And took him riding in the air!

226

Up above the tree-tops,
   Caught in the crackling wood,
Benjamin kept shouting,
   "All things work together for good!"

"Be brave, my friend, all's well!"
   Shouted dear old Grandpa Mole;
Then whispered to himself,
   "Hmmm…but *I'm* safe in this hole!"

"It's easy cheering down there,"
   Benjamin gave a shout;
"It's hard to see that all is well
   Up here in this roundabout!"

"WOO-AH!" — the big wind roared again,
   And Benjamin flew higher,
Soaring past Grandpa Mole's balloon
   In his tumbleweed high-flyer!

227

Then snap, crack, crunch and whirling,
  The tumbleweed plunged down
On Mrs. Mouse's small green lawn,
  At the other side of town.

The lawn was filled with leaves
  That the wind had blown in there;
Mrs. Mouse was squeaking,
  "This is more than I can bear."

But quickly snatching, catching,
  Benjamin rolled around,
Gathering leaves on every point,
  'Til not one was left on the ground!

Then off again on the gusty wind,
  In his giant tumbleweed,
Benjamin rode as the captain
  Of his trusty, clean-up steed.

MRS.
MOUSE

Rolling, blowing through the clouds,
　　And turning end on end,
Benjamin heard Mrs. Mouse
　　Calling, "Thank you, friend!"

"Well, that's one deed I helped with
　　That sheds light upon this verse,
'All things work together for good…'
　　Even when things seem worse!"

"Oh, what is this that's flying
　　Like a yellow-handled sail?
I do believe it must be
　　Charlie Cricket's own air mail!"

"My tumbleweed can save it
　　With a crackly, wooden snag."
And reaching very quickly,
　　Benjamin caught the lost mail bag.

HUFF! PUFF! A cloud blew round him,
  And he couldn't see at all
Where the wind was blowing him.
  He felt so lost and small.

He didn't see the mail bag
  Fall down from the tumbleweed,
And drop at Charlie Cricket's feet
  As fast as air-mail speed.

"Thank you, thank you," Charlie cried,
  "You're the hero of the day.
The letters are all saved,
  When I thought they'd blown away!"

"A hero, really, am I?
  While I'm tossed and blown about?
I cannot understand this,
  And that's without a doubt!"

"Well...I'll think of something hopeful
   While I'm in this fluffy cloud;
I know! I'll say my verse again,
   And shout it very loud!"

"All things work together for good
   To those who love the Lord;
All things work together for good
   To those who love the Lord!"

He shouted to the big wind,
   "I will safely land — and soon!"
When all at once he felt
   The ropes of Grandpa Mole's balloon.

He hung on tightly to one end,
   As the cloud was blown away;
Then suddenly — the wind was still;
   He began to gently sway.

Softly, softly, he floated down;
　Such a funny sight was he,
Inside a tumbleweed balloon
　Over Dandelion Sea.

Grandpa Mole was cheering him
　For saving his balloon;
While Lucy Ladybug
　Played him a "Happy Landing" tune.

"Dear Benjamin! You've landed!
　What adventures you've withstood;
And I heard you shouting in the air,
　'All things work together for good!'"

232

"Yes, dear Grandpa Mole, that's true,
  But before I blew away,
I didn't know those words would fit
  The things that happened today."

"It's hard for just a bumblebee
  To learn in one short day,
But I believe these words are true,
  And I'll understand someday, how:

  'All things work
  Together for good
  To those who
  Love the Lord!'"

BECAUSE JESUS LIVES

Little seeds can grow like this,
Because Jesus lives!

Little eggs can hatch a chick,
Because Jesus lives!

The sun can shine upon my face,
Because Jesus lives!

A bird can find its way through space,
Because Jesus lives!

I can feel the ocean's spray,
Because Jesus lives!

God will hear me when I pray,
Because Jesus lives!

I can pick the golden rod,
Because Jesus lives!

I can go to live with God,
Because Jesus lives!

STAR LIGHT, STAR BRIGHT

Star light, star bright,
  Guide us on our way tonight;
I wish I may, I wish I might,
  See the King this very night.

NOW I LAY ME DOWN TO
SLEEP

Now I lay me down to sleep,
 I pray the Lord my soul to keep;
I know He watches over me,
 So I can sleep as safe can be!

SHALL WE GO A-SHARING?

"Old woman, old woman,
  Shall we go a-sharing?"
"Speak a little louder, sir,
  I'm very hard of hearing."
"Old woman, old woman,
  I love you very dearly."
"Thank you very kindly, sir,
  I hear you very clearly."

238

SNAIL, SNAIL

Snail, Snail,
Put out your horns,
Be glad! Be glad!
Don't be forlorn.
The trees clap hands,
The hills, they sing!
Don't you hear
The bluebells ring?
Come and join them!
Ring-a-ling!
God cares for us!
Come! Sing! Sing! Sing!

DANDELION SEA SUMMER GAMES

Do you hear the music
  In Dandelion Sea?
It's time for Summer Games;
  Would you like to come with me?

There is such excitement,
  With bands and flags and noise!
It's a grand occasion
  For watching, girls and boys!

There's racing, flying, diving,
  And fun for everyone;
Look! They're giving medals.
  Listen! Let's see who won!

240

"Ladies and gentlemen,
Our judges agree
On these champions
At Dandelion Sea!"...

"The longest non-stop flight gold medal
Goes to Billy-Boy Blue Goose!
Sixteen hundred miles he flew —
Without a wing getting loose!"

199 FT.

200 FT.

"The champion of diving
Is Emperor Pat Penguin,
Who went down over two hundred feet —
A big gold medal to win!"

"The fastest bird we timed today
Is the zooming, Spine-tailed Swift;
Over one hundred miles an hour!
A gold medal for you, Swifty-Swift!"

"Boys and girls, let's stop to cheer
The power of God, indeed,
Who makes His creatures fly and dive,
Without a motor for speed!"

"Well…
What is this group over here,
Singing in the oak tree shade?
Hello, Bright-Bill! What's the meaning
Of this Summer Games parade?"

242

"We're having a celebration,
  Though we didn't win medals today;
Stay and listen as we thank God
  For what we enjoy *every* day!"

Katy Kangaroo said…
  "I will thank Him for my pouch,
  Where all my babies ride and crouch!"

Mickey Monkey said…
  "I will thank Him for my tail,
  From which I hang, and swing and sail!"

Peter Pelican said…
  "I will thank Him for my sack,
  Where fishes for my lunch I pack!"

Tommy Turtle said…
"I will thank Him for my shell,
That makes a house that I love well!"

Mary Meadowlark said…
"I will thank Him for my song,
That makes you happy all day long!"

Sherry Sheep said…
"I will thank Him for my fleece,
That makes a boy's coat, piece by piece!"

"Boys and girls…
The Bible says:
'Let everything that has breath
Praise the Lord!'

So…
If penguins, pelicans, turtles, too,
Can all be thankful —
HOW ABOUT YOU!"

244

A ROBIN AND A ROBIN'S SON

A robin and a robin's son,
 Once went to town to buy a bun.
They couldn't decide
 On plum or plain,
And so they went back home again.

Then robin and the robin's son,
 Decided to agree on plum.
So back to town
 They went once more,
And wished they had agreed before!

WATCH!

Watch the little silkworms spin;
   Watch the squirrels gathering in
Nuts for winter's food to share,
   Telling friends, "Prepare! Prepare!"

Watch the dormouse make a bed;
   Watch the spider spin his thread,
Weaving webs with utmost care,
   Telling friends, "Prepare! Prepare!"

Watch the ants go scurrying by;
  Watch the bees as on they fly,
Gathering pollen here and there,
  Telling friends, "Prepare! Prepare!"

"Watch!" The Lord says, "watch the sky!
  Watch for Jesus' trumpet cry."
Boys and girls from everywhere,
  Telling friends, "Prepare! Prepare!"

247

BETTY BOTTER

Betty Botter did but mutter,
   "But," she said, " the mutter's bitter;
If I'm bitter while I mutter,
   It will fill my heart with clutter;
But a bit of better chatter,
   That would make my heart feel better."
So she sought some words to fit her,
   Which were kind instead of bitter;
Soon she sang and didn't mutter,
   So kept out that awful clutter;
So 'twas better Betty Botter
   Changed from bitter things to better!

DIDDLE, DIDDLE, DUMPLING

Diddle, diddle, dumpling,
  My son John,
Prayed in bed
  With his stockings on;
The angels laughed,
  And peeped, one by one,
To see John praying
  With his stockings on.

Diddle, diddle, dumpling,
  My son John,
Sang and praised
  With no stockings on!
Ten little toes
  Praising God's dear Son;
Diddle, diddle, dumpling,
  My son John.

DOCTOR FOSTER

Doctor Foster went to Gloucester
In a shower of rain;
He went to teach,
He went to preach
God's Word, and make it plain.

LITTLE NANCY ETTICOAT

Little Nancy Etticoat
  In a white petticoat,
With a little light
  That glows and glows!
Never tries to hide it;
  All the town has spied it!
Little Nancy Etticoat's
  Little light grows!

A DILLAR, A DOLLAR

A dillar, a dollar,
  A ten o'clock scholar,
He's on time for his church school!
  He got up early in the morning
To keep the Golden Rule:
  "Love the Lord
  With all your heart,
  And all your playmates, too!"
A dillar, a dollar,
  A ten o'clock scholar,
God is watching over you!

YOU ARE SPECIAL

You are very, very special;
    There is no one just like you!
God made you just the way you are,
    When He specially thought of you.
He wanted so many children,
    And not one to be the same,
So that you could be a special you,
    With a very special name.
So He put a special mark upon your feet,
    And fingers, too!
And of all the children everywhere
    No one has that mark, but you!
So, smile your very special smile,
    And give Dad your special squeeze.
Help Mommy with your special hands,
    (And it's special to say,
    "Thank you," and "Please.").
Then to every SPECIAL little girl,
    And every SPECIAL little boy,
God has given a SPECIAL HEART
    To put His love in to enjoy.

THE BELLS OF LONDON

Oranges and lemons,
Say the Bells of St. Clements;

God made big red apples,
   Say the Bells of Whitechapel;

He made rain and snow
   Says the big Bell of Bow;

The world's in His hands
   Say the Bells of St. Anne's;

He never will fail me
   Say the bells of Old Bailey;

Crown Him with Crowns,
   Say the bells over town.

Ding, dong, ding, dong;
Ding, dong, ding, dong.
Crown Him with Crowns
Say the bells over town.

THE SMILEY SAROO

High up in a swing
  In Tinkertoy Town,
A boy named Bobby
  Just started to frown.

But a funny bird,
  Called a Smiley Saroo,
Pulled up Bobby's lips
  And Bobby smiled, too!

Now, a Smiley Saroo
  Has a smile you can catch,
And wherever he goes
  Children smile, by the batch!

It is said that the smiles
   He started in town,
Have chased away hundreds
   And hundreds of frowns.

He began with a boy
   Who caught the first smile;
Then a girl caught one, too!
   And passed on a big pile.

And before you knew it,
   Why! Folks everywhere,
Had all caught the smiles
   And were smiling out there.

From our house to your house
   And over the hill,
There are long lines of smiles
   That keep catching on, still!

And that Smiley Saroo
   Who started the smiles,
Has now covered the world
   With his smiles-by-the-miles.

THE JOLLY MILLER

There was a Jolly Miller
  Who lived by the River Dee;
He worked and sang while baking bread,
  A happy man was he.

One day he baked a loaf so big,
  The best he'd ever seen;
"I should never sell this loaf," said he,
  "But wrap it and keep it clean."

He put it on his wooden cart,
  And wheeled it right along;
And as he pushed it to his home
  He sang his miller song:

"Oh, I'm a Jolly Miller,
And I bake some jolly bread,
So that all the jolly people
Can be jolly-well, well-fed."

FRESH
BREAD

Just then, he passed a lassie,
  Who was Mrs. Sarah's daughter;
She was singing, oh, so sweetly,
  "Cast your bread upon the water."

"Cast your bread upon the water,
Cast your bread upon the water,
Cast your bread upon the water,
  It will come back twice as big!"

The Jolly Miller stopped his cart,
  And wondered at what she said!
"Did she mean that I should cast away
  My biggest and best loaf of bread?"

"Young lady, now, I ask you,
  Why do you sing such a song?
To throw my bread into the river
  Might be very, very wrong."

Now, Mrs. Sarah's daughter,
  Who could sing just like a bird,
Replied, "My dear Jolly Miller,
  I am singing from God's Word."

"It is written in the Bible
  If we give our bread away,
God will bless it and then bring
  It back again, someday."

"If God has written it,
    Then it's true," the Jolly Miller sighed.
So he turned his wooden cart around
    And went to the riverside.

With a little tear in his jolly eye,
    He tipped his cart by a tree;
And that big loaf of bread
    Went bob-bob-bobbing down the River Dee.

It bobbed along all day and night
    'Til it came to Dandelion Sea,
Where Charlie Cricket, the town's mailman,
    Saw it first and said, "Gracious me!"

He ran with his mail to Mrs. Mouse,
    Then to Grandfather Mole he sped;
"Come quickly and see what has floated in!
    It's a mountain of golden bread!"

Before you could say, "Fee-Fi-Fo-Fum,"
  The news went through all the town.
And as the sun came up, from each house and street
  Came little creatures in nightcaps and gowns.

Then Brother Rabbit came hopping by
  And said, "Well, bless the Lord!
This is enough bread for all of us,
  And much more than we could afford!"

"Bring your baskets and fill to the top.
  No one need go hungry," he said;
"And God bless the man, wherever he is,
  Who sent this wonderful bread."

So all the town of Dandelion Sea
  Went home to breakfast, to dine
On golden pieces of crusty bread,
  That gleamed like bright sunshine.

When Sidney Squirrel and his friends
   Had filled each hollow tree,
The loaf of bread grew big again,
   And went bobbing out to sea.

It sailed along to Blossom Bay,
   Then down to Chipmunk Chigger,
And everytime it fed a town,
   It sailed away much bigger!

At last it came back to the town
  Beside the River Dee.
The Jolly Miller at his work
  Said, "What is this I see?"

"My loaf of bread is twice as big!"
  Then he ran out of the door,
And laughed and clapped his jolly hands,
  And sang his song as before:

"Oh, I'm a Jolly Miller,
And with this big loaf of bread,
All the jolly, jolly people
Can be jolly-well, well-fed!"

BYE, BABY BUNTING

Bye, baby bunting,
  Mother's gone a-hunting,
To get a bulrush basket skin
  To hide the baby bunting in.

TEN LITTLE MISSIONARIES

GO YE INTO ALL THE WORLD WITH GOOD NEWS! GOOD NEWS!

Ten little missionaries,
   Holding up a sign;
One went to Zanzibar,
   Then there were nine!

Nine little missionaries
   Learning to translate;
One went to Washington,
   Then there were eight!

Eight little missionaries
  Looking up to Heaven;
One went to the Isle of Man,
  Then there were seven!

Seven little missionaries,
  Building with red bricks;
One became a farmer,
  Then there were six!

Six little missionaries,
    To the woods arrive;
One went back home again,
    Then there were five!

Five little missionaries,
    On a lake shore;
One went to mend a net,
    Then there were four!

266

Four little missionaries,
  Singing happily;
One went to tell Good News,
  Then there were three!

Three little missionaries,
  Praying what to do;
One went to his friend's house,
  Then there were two!

Two little missionaries,
    Sailing to Ceylon;
One got off at Egypt,
    Then there was one!

One little missionary,
    Praising God's dear Son;
Flew into the clouds,
    And then there were none!

RUB-A-DUB-DUB

Rub-a-dub-dub,
  Three boys in a tub,
Getting as clean as can be.
  Rubbing and scrubbing,
And scrubbing and rubbing,
  To please their mommy, you see.

THE ANT

I would not crush
  A little ant
That hurries through the grass,
  For God spent time
To make him;
  So I shall let him pass.

PUSSY-CAT, PUSSY-CAT

Pussy-cat, Pussy-cat,
  Where have you been?
I've been to Sheba
  To see the Queen.
Pussy-cat, Pussy-cat,
  What did you there?
I crept in to listen
  Under her chair.

Pussy-cat, Pussy-cat,
  What did she say?
She said she had traveled
  A long, long way.
Pussy-cat, Pussy-cat,
  Where did she go?
To Solomon's land
  With gifts to bestow.

Pussy-cat, Pussy-cat,
  What did she see?
A great, famous King,
  Wise and glorious was he.
Pussy-cat, Pussy-cat,
  Is her tale bold?
No! She said that the half
  Has not yet been told!

270

AS I WAS GOING TO ST. IVES

As I was going to St. Ives,
I met a man with seven cows.
Each cow was strong and fat,
But seven thin cows came after that.
Then came seven fat ears of corn,
Next came seven ears, thin and worn.
  Cows - thin! Cows - fat!
  Ears - thin! Ears - fat!
Who was the man who dreamed all that?

BOBBING THINGS

Bobbing things are everywhere!
  Duck tails bobbing, by the pair;
Bottles corked upon the sea;
  Apples in a tub, for me!
Robins bobbing on the ground;
  Bobbing things are all around!

Bobbing things are everywhere!
  Land or sea, or in the air;
But the nicest bobbing sight,
  Around the world, and every night,
Is heads-a-bobbing in sweet prayer;
  Yes, bobbing heads are everywhere!

PEAS IN A POD

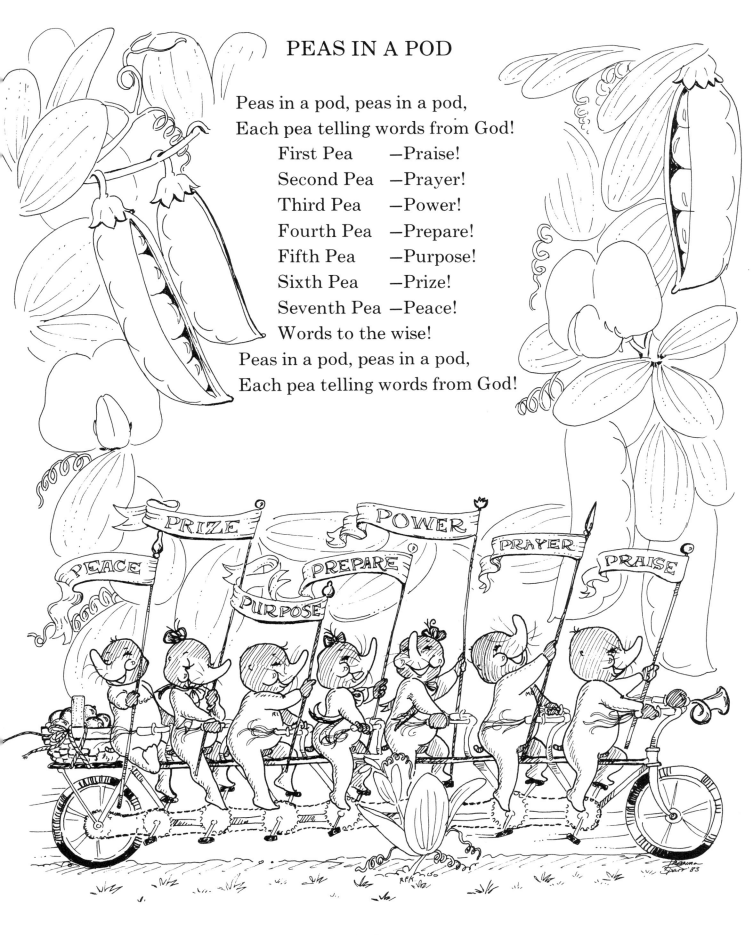

Peas in a pod, peas in a pod,
Each pea telling words from God!

First Pea	—Praise!
Second Pea	—Prayer!
Third Pea	—Power!
Fourth Pea	—Prepare!
Fifth Pea	—Purpose!
Sixth Pea	—Prize!
Seventh Pea	—Peace!

Words to the wise!
Peas in a pod, peas in a pod,
Each pea telling words from God!

273

THE NOOKS AND CRANNIES

In the Nooks and Crannies,
    Live the Gramps and Grannies,
So wise in years and thought;
    All the reams of words
    They have learned and heard,
They sift, and save, and sort.

They are very thrifty,
    And are very swifty
To use words that are the best;
    To select each word
    That is preferred,
They prepare a simple test.

They will chew and savor
    Every word's own flavor,
And their taste buds tell the tale;
    They can tell what's sweet,
    And what's good to eat,
And what's sour, and cross, and stale.

274

With such fine selection,
  Their condensed collection
Of wisdom is like pure gold;
  Each word is seasoned
  With salt, and reasoned
To be shared with each household.

So the Gramps and Grannies,
  In the Nooks and Crannies,
Arrange words in small lots.
  They write them on scrolls,
  And bake them in rolls,
And store them away in pots.

It is said that some Gramps,
  Who could chew words like champs,
Gained fame by words that were few;
  And a quiet Granny,
  With wisdom uncanny,
Reduced ten words to just two!

275

For the Gramps and Grannies,
  In the Nooks and Crannies,
Remember short proverbs well;
  And have passed them on down,
  Winning much renown
From wise and good words they tell.

Today they are baking
  The rolls they are taking
To join the Feast, with their friends;
  They'll stuff all the rolls,
  With "good advice" scrolls,
They've practiced, and preached and penned.

The rolls that are rising
  Smell most appetizing,
And Grannies have stuffed them well,
  With, "Birds of a feather
  Flock together,"
And, "Time and tide will tell."

The rolls nearly done,
  Say, "Like father, like son,"
And, "A stitch in time saves nine."
  While those on the shelf
  Are stuffed, "Health is wealth,"
And, "Let your little light shine."

The rolls extra crusty,
  Are filled with words trusty:
"Wisdom is better than gold."
  And, "A friend in need
  Is a friend indeed."
"The half has not yet been told!"

In double-roll hollows,
  A double scroll follows
The shape of the double bun;
  "Two wrongs don't make right,"
  Is baked in there, tight,
With, "Two heads are better than one."

A Little Child Shall Lead Them

The rolls Gramps are stacking,
  And Grannies are packing,
Say, "Love will cover all things."
  And those on a tray,
  Being carried away,
Say, "I will trust under His wings."

Now the Gramps and Grannies,
  From the Nooks and Crannies,
Are off to the Feast, God-speed them!
  With a cart load of rolls,
  And a banner with scrolls:
" A little child shall lead them."

277

HOT CROSS BUNS

Hot cross buns,
Hot cross buns,
One a penny,
Two a penny,
Hot cross buns.
Give them to your daughters,
Give them to your sons,
Tell them Who's The Bread of Life!
Hot cross buns.

278

THE NORTH WIND DOTH BLOW

The north wind doth blow,
And we shall have snow,
And what will poor robin do then?
Poor thing.
He'll sit in a barn,
And keep himself warm,
And wait for God's sunshine and spring,
Wise thing!

WHAT IF?

What if?...
We never knew
If we jumped in the air,
Whether we would come down
Right away, or next year!

What if?...
The sun might rise,
And then it might not.
And icicles chilly,
Were sometimes red hot!

What if?...
The rain rained *up*,
And once a year, *down!*
And smiles could get loose,
And turn into frowns!

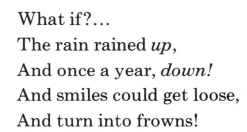

What if?...
Once in a while
The corn came up peas!
And all of the seeds
Had no guarantees!

What if?...
Suddenly, cows
Gave pink lemonade!
And sometimes the lemons
Grew dark purple shade!

What if?…
The moon might shine,
And then it might not.
And bees made no honey,
Because they forgot!

What if?…
A day at times
Turned two days instead!
And springtime arrived
In December ahead!

What if?…
The tide went out,
But never came in!
And sometimes the earth
Would go for a spin!

But…
Thank you, dear Lord,
You rule earth and space,
And order aright
Everything in its place!

281

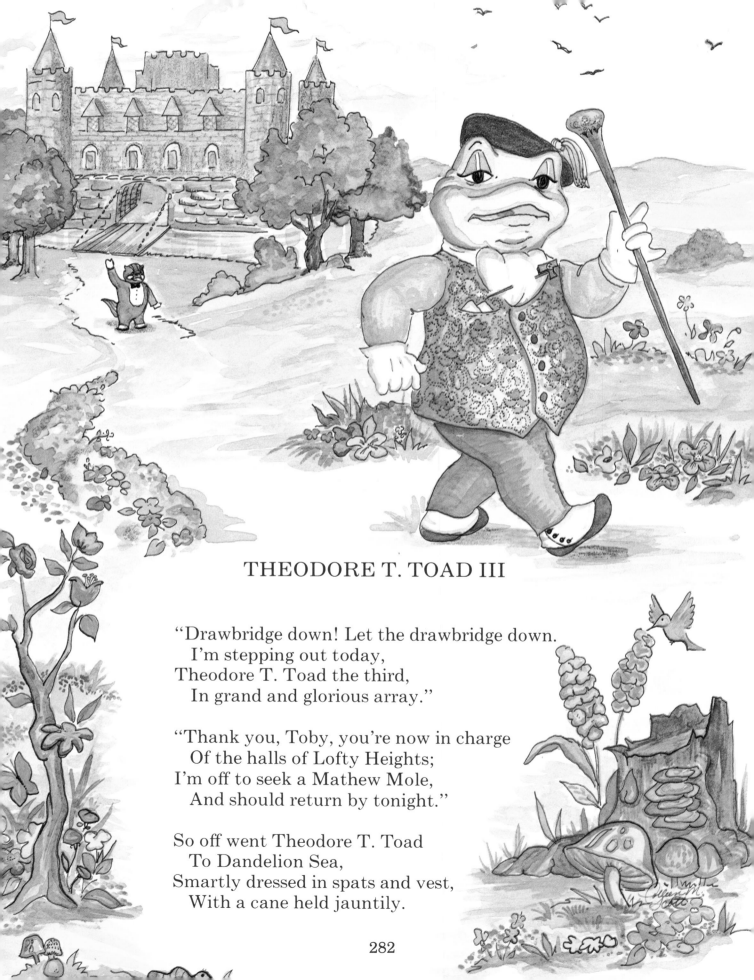

THEODORE T. TOAD III

"Drawbridge down! Let the drawbridge down.
   I'm stepping out today,
Theodore T. Toad the third,
   In grand and glorious array."

"Thank you, Toby, you're now in charge
   Of the halls of Lofty Heights;
I'm off to seek a Mathew Mole,
   And should return by tonight."

So off went Theodore T. Toad
   To Dandelion Sea,
Smartly dressed in spats and vest,
   With a cane held jauntily.

Strutting along the winding path,
　And through the leafy roads,
He sang his favorite walking song,
　"I Am Not As Other Toads."

By ten, he reached the meadow's edge
　At Humpty Dumpty's wall,
And carefully climbed the rocky steps
　So that he would not fall.

"Good morning, Humpty Dumpty, sir;
　How amazing, you're still here!
By legend, you were shattered,
　Now cohesive you appear."

Humpty jumped, and said with a smile,
　"The tale of 'Horses and Men,'
Wasn't the end! The KING HIMSELF,
　Put me together again!"

"Miracles still occur, I'm told,"
　Theodore began to extol,
"But please be so kind to direct me
　To a certain Mathew Mole."

"Keep walking on the meadow path,
　You'll find good help, Mr. Toad,
From neighbors going to the Feast,
　Who'll direct you on the road."

283

Toad saw Mary and her lamb,
　Who were walking up ahead,
With Tommy Tucker pushing mounds
　Of golden barley bread.

They cheerfully directed Toad
　To pass the Old-Shoe House,
Then follow signs near the cottage
　Marked, "Danny D. Dormouse."

Quite soon, Toad reached the little spot
　Where Charlie Cricket lunched;
"Good-day, Mr. Cricket, pardon my
　Intrusion while you munch."

"Is this perchance the rustic road
　To Dandelion Sea?"
Charlie answered, "Indeed, it is.
　You're a stranger here, I see."

"Of course! I live across the moat,
　In splendid Lofty Heights;
I'm Theodore T. Toad the third,
　From a line of titled knights."

"I'm Charlie Cricket, Mr. Toad,
　And the happy mailman here;
Are you related to Stubmie Toad,
　Our surveyor-engineer?"

"Please observe, I'm a high-born Toad,
　　Well versed in law, and refined;
Such toads as Stubmie Toad can't be
　　Related to *my* toads' kind."

"I see, Mr. Toad, quite clearly,
　　You're not from these parts at all,
So may I ask what brings you here,
　　And to what do we owe your call?"

"I'm seeking out a Mathew Mole,
　　Who wears a watch, I hear,
That fits a Lofty Heights heirloom
　　That's been lost for many a year."

"Mathew Mole! he's my best friend;
　　A gentleman, good and kind.
He's better known as Grandpa Mole,
　　The most honest mole you'll find."

"How far then is it to his house?"
　　Toad asked, "which is the way?"
Charlie replied, "Follow that sign;
　　It's seventy-five hops by survey."

"Seventy-five hops! How far is *that*?
　　Such survey sounds quite silly.
Did Stubmie Toad use standards hops,
　　Or metric hops, or milli?"

Charlie smiled, "It's not so far;
　　I'll take you, if you like."
"No, thank you," Toad said, walking off,
　　"I prefer a *private* hike."

He rambled on through yellow flowers,
　　"Tut-tutting" all the time,
When all at once he heard a voice
　　Say, "Children, here's a rhyme."

"Twinkle, twinkle, little star,
God has placed you where you are;
Up above the world so high,
You're God's light hung in the sky."

"Great cackling figments! Mother Goose!"
　　He puffed around a bend,
Seeing Mother Goose upon a log
　　Reciting to her friends.

"Madam, what pure simplicity;
　　Such unscholastic bliss.
The minds of children should be primed
　　By versions such as this:

"Scintillate, scintillate,
Stellar diminutive;
Deity hath established
Thine abode, definitive.
Pre-eminently poised
Aloft terrestrial,
Deity's illumination
Suspended—celestial!"

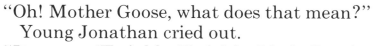

"Oh! Mother Goose, what does that mean?"
  Young Jonathan cried out.
"It means, 'Twinkle, Twinkle, Little Star,'
  With the words turned inside-out."

"My version quite escapes the minds
  Of this fair wonderland,"
Theodore said, "but I commend
  Its friendly, helping hands."

"I'm on my way to Mathew Mole
  Who lives around this section;
Please inform me if I'm correct
  In taking this direction."

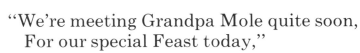

"We're meeting Grandpa Mole quite soon,
  For our special Feast today,"
Mother Goose smiled. "Perhaps you'd like
  To join us on the way."

"A special Feast? And what about?"
  Theodore asked in surprise.
"A Feast to rejoice in God's great love,"
  Little Jane, with smiles, replied.

"What quaint traditions you have here
  In Dandelion Sea,"
Theodore sighed, "but I extend
  My thanks for inviting me."

"Goodbye, Mother Goose and children,"
  Then strutting off once more,
Theodore and his walking song
  Performed a fine encore.

287

Arriving at the meadow's edge,
  He spied Mole's house beyond;
"Ah-hah! I've found you, watch and all,"
  He called across the pond.

Just as he knocked at Mole's front door,
  He heard a chuckling voice,
Singing somewhere from underground,
  "Sorrabahum!" and "Rejoice!"

Theodore crept to the hole nearby,
  Where the singing swirled about;
And peering in, came face to face
  With Mole who was coming out!

Their noses touched, meeting eye to eye,
  "Mathew Mole, sir, I presume.
I'm Theodore T. Toad the third."
  Grandpa Mole said, "Sorrabahum!"

"Sorrabahum? Now, what is that?
  A local word, no doubt."
"That's how a mole says, 'Bless you,'"
  Grandpa Mole said, climbing out.

Putting down his juice for the Feast,
  Mole smiled, "Now, years ago,
My grandfather knew *your* grandfather,
  Our family records show."

"*My* grandfather knew *your* grandfather!
    That's not our custom today.
You live in a hole, Mr. Mole;
    A mansion's my home, by the way."

Mole quietly quoted: "It's better
    To dwell in a hole in the ground,
    Where there's love,
    Than to dwell in a mansion
    Where love and contentment's not found."

"Oh, dear, what quaint little proverbs
    You people know in these parts,"
Theodore said. "Now my mission
    I'd like to conclude, then depart."

"The gold watch you're wearing, Mr. Mole,
    Belongs in *our* collection;
A fine antique—missing many years—
    That was lost in Boat-Bay section."

"That's where my grandfather found this watch!
    And passed it down with care;
Most ordinary moles never have
    Such a fine, gold watch to wear."

"I'm prepared to give you, Mr. Mole,
    Five hundred coins to buy back
This priceless heirloom," Theodore said,
    While jingling the gold in a sack.

"I cannot accept all your money,"
    Grandpa Mole, with tears, replied;
As sadly he took off the heirloom
    He'd worn twenty years with pride.

"Mr. Toad, I have just one request;
    Going home, kindly stop and read
The message engraved inside that watch,
    That must be your family's creed."

"I give you my word, Mr. Mole,
    Since you have been honest and fair,
That on the way home I will ponder
    The message my family left there."

"Goodbye, Mr. Mole, and I thank you."
    "Goodbye, Mr. Toad, I'll now leave
For the Feast of Rejoicing—but somehow—
    This will all work for good, I believe."

So Toad walked back through the meadow,
    Success now quickened his pace;
Rubbing and shining the fine gold watch,
    Till he stopped to open the case.

Only five words were engraved there,
    But those words gave Toad a shock;
He read, "Love thy neighbor as thyself,"
    Then gasped, and fell over a rock!

The fine gold watch flew through the air,
    And Theodore landed in pain;
"Help! Help, someone! Oh, my ankle;
    I've suffered an awful sprain!"

290

Charlie Cricket came running by,
  And said, "What happened to you?"
"I tripped and stumbled on that rock,"
  Moaned Theodore, black and blue.

"The *best* of toads can take a fall,"
  Wise Charlie gently spoke;
"I'll see that you get into town
  For help from friendly folk."

Then Charlie helped Theodore get up,
  And hobbling off together,
Theodore's pain made him forget
  The watch—in a clump of heather!

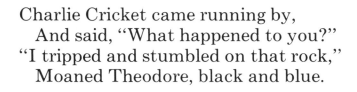

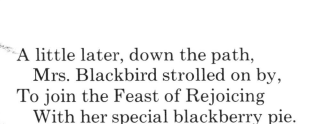

A little later, down the path,
  Mrs. Blackbird strolled on by,
To join the Feast of Rejoicing
  With her special blackberry pie.

Her keen eyes saw the fine gold watch;
  "That's Grandpa Mole's!" she cried.
"He must have lost it—I'll take it back."
  So she ran with longer stride.

Then Mrs. Blackbird, watch, and pie,
  Went on to meet her friends,
Quite unaware she plays a part
  In how this story ends.

But, oh, it's the Feast of Rejoicing!
  When things should be made right.
Be very sure, we'll meet Mr. Toad,
  Grandpa Mole, and the watch before night.

291

I SAW A SHIP A-SAILING

I saw a ship a-sailing,
   A-sailing on the sea;
And, oh, but it was laden
   With happy gifts for Thee!

There was singing in the cabin,
   And praising in the hold;
The sails were made of linen,
   And the masts were made of gold.

There were gifts in little boxes,
   And gifts in treasure chests;
Candlesticks and apples,
   With spices—just the best!

And precious little vessels
   Were neatly packed aboard;
The flags were flying high,
   "Cheery Givers to The Lord!"

The decks were filled with children,
   A-sailing off so brave;
And tanks of thanks were bobbing
   Up and down with every wave.

The captain was a father,
   A gallant, cheery chap;
And when the ship began to move
   The children cheered and clapped!

THEODORE T. TOAD RETURNS

The table is all ready
   In Polly-Woggle Park,
Brother Rabbit will be host,
   From afternoon to dark.

Grandpa Mole is helping him
   To set the juice in place;
Everyone will soon arrive,
   And greet with fond embrace.

For all of Dandelion Sea
   Looks forward, once a year,
To meeting friends on Feast Day,
   In God's love and friendship dear.

Brother Rabbit checked the time;
   "I'll miss your watch," he said
To Grandpa Mole, who nodded,
   "Well, it's Theodore's now, instead."

"That watch will soon be hanging
   In the halls of Lofty Heights,
And rightly so, it came from there,
   And should be back tonight."

"I see the first arrivals
   Coming down the meadow road,"
Brother Rabbit looked—then cried,
   "Oh dear, it's Mr. Toad!"

Theodore came with limp and groan,
   On Charlie Cricket's shoulder;
"I fell, while looking in that watch;
   My ankle struck a boulder."

Grandpa Mole said, "Sit right here,
    We'll bandage up the sprain,
And help you get back safely
    With your watch, back home again."

"The watch, the watch, I've lost it!"
    Theodore suddenly realized.
"I hurt so much I quite forgot
    My priceless, heirloom prize."

"How sad, but we'll help find it,"
    Grandpa Mole assured poor Toad,
As Mrs. Blackbird rushed to them
    With, "See my precious load?"

"We'll gather willing hands,"
    Grandpa Mole said, cheerily,
"To get you back to Lofty Heights;
    Stay! Share the Feast with me."

"Grandpa Mole, I found your watch
    Along the meadow road."
"Thank you, but that watch belongs
    To Theodore T. Toad."

"How kind and honest, Madam,
    To return it," Theodore spoke;
"But far more precious is my foot,
    And help from kindly folk."

"Grandpa Mole, your kind request
    I do accept herein,"
Said Theodore, settling on a log,
    To watch the Feast begin.

And that's how Mr. Toad became
    The unexpected guest,
At Polly-Woggle Park that day,
    Which changed things for the best.

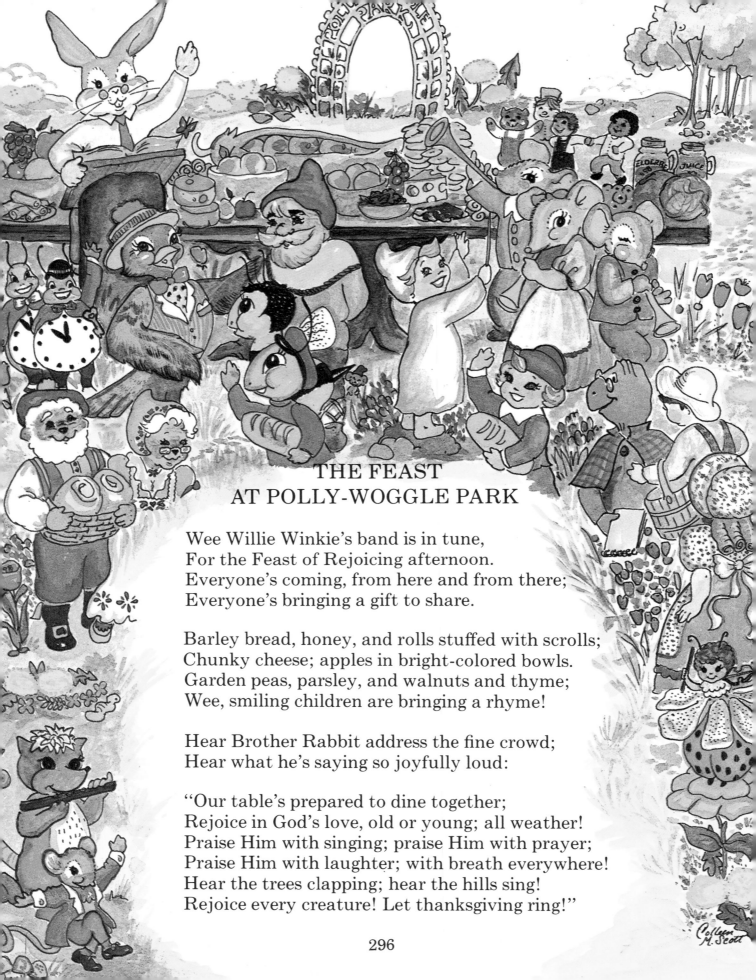

THE FEAST
AT POLLY-WOGGLE PARK

Wee Willie Winkie's band is in tune,
For the Feast of Rejoicing afternoon.
Everyone's coming, from here and from there;
Everyone's bringing a gift to share.

Barley bread, honey, and rolls stuffed with scrolls;
Chunky cheese; apples in bright-colored bowls.
Garden peas, parsley, and walnuts and thyme;
Wee, smiling children are bringing a rhyme!

Hear Brother Rabbit address the fine crowd;
Hear what he's saying so joyfully loud:

"Our table's prepared to dine together;
Rejoice in God's love, old or young; all weather!
Praise Him with singing; praise Him with prayer;
Praise Him with laughter; with breath everywhere!
Hear the trees clapping; hear the hills sing!
Rejoice every creature! Let thanksgiving ring!"

Happy, small creatures in this pleasant land,
Cheered Brother Rabbit with clapping of hands,
But off to the side, one thoughtful face showed
His heart had been touched—Theodore T. Toad!
Theodore then whispered in Mother Goose's ear;
She smiled with delight at such kind words to hear.

Then taking his watch, and holding it high,
She announced to all, "It's with pleasure that I
Present this gift to the Feast celebration,
From Theodore T. Toad's entire generation.
The watch he has given to grace the household
Of our friend and counselor, Grandpa Mole!"

Everyone cheered with, "Hip, hip, hurray!"
And the band joined in with a trumpet display;
Till the whole land rang with the cheery voicing,
On the wonderful day of the Feast of Rejoicing!

297

INDEX OF BIG BOOK THEMES

INDEX OF BIG BOOK THEMES

Storyteller's Note

"We spend our years as a tale that is told..."

My tale begins in Liverpool, England. As a little girl, I played and romped to the strains of old Mother Goose rhymes on worn cobblestone streets; dancing rhymes, riddle rhymes, game rhymes, and counting rhymes. It was far from my mind, then, that one day the tale of *Christian Mother Goose* would be written in far-away America — the America I grew to love as a young war bride transplanted from the shores of England.

The Christian Mother Goose story began in the Rocky Mountain regions of Colorado...in a bathtub! It was a favorite place of mine to soak and study at the end of a busy day, usually crowded with the amazing adventures of raising four sons.

Walkie-Talkies had just appeared. Ahh!...what a boon! I could now fill the demand for bedtime stories from the bathtub, while the boys listened eagerly with their Walkie-Talkies tucked beneath their pillows. Original stories were woven nightly from the "soak and send" station. And it was there in the bath bubbles, studying the Bible, and catching a glimpse of an old Mother Goose book on the floor, that the inspiration for *Christian* Mother Goose was born. It was a curiously appropriate combination of my long-time love of God's Word, and my on-going quest into the mysteries of old Mother Goose.

I thought of the Scripture, "By my God have I leaped over a wall." And, indeed, over a wall I *did* leap! — with scores of Bible themes and Scriptural truths to clothe scores of rhymes in that whimsical world that has influenced all of us to some degree — the nostalgic world of nursery rhyme.

From the ancient village of Canterbury to the historic town of Gloucester; from Shakespeare to Charles Dickens; from the British Parliament to Wrigley's chewing gum empire, Mother Goose rhymes have scripted many a human drama.

I have frequently come upon Bible passages that bring those old rhyming themes to bear: "I will go before thee, and make the crooked places straight." The "Crooked Man" immediately comes to mind. "When I fall, I shall arise..." A perfect promise for the heretofore hopeless Humpty Dumpty. My Bible is earmarked with similar associations. I have listed many of them in the Christian Mother Goose Rock-A-Bye Bible.

Here, in the Christian Mother Goose BIG BOOK, you will find the most complete Collection of the best-known rhymes, along with parables, brought together in this large, Gift Edition.

It is my prayer that this Collection will lead little children everywhere, to know Him, The Author of the greatest "Once upon a time..." story every told; the story of the amazing grace and love of God, in The Lord Jesus Christ.

300

About the Author ...
MARJORIE AINSBOROUGH DECKER

#1 National Bestselling Author, Marjorie Ainsborough Decker is well-known and loved as one of America's most heart-warming storytellers.

A native of Liverpool, England, Mrs. Decker now resides in the United States with her husband Dale. They are parents of four grown sons.

Her Christian Mother Goose® Classics have endeared the trust of parents and the twinkle of children around the world.

Along with authoring twelve books in the Christian Mother Goose® Series, Marjorie Decker, a respected Adult Conference Speaker, combines genuine enthusiasm and colorful storytelling skills with sound Biblical scholarship. There is a pleasant nostalgia to her children's books with a curious appeal to Bible lovers of all ages.

Mrs. Decker's charming adventures — her books' characters, illustrated stories and well-known rhymes — lift the spirit, quicken the mind, and stir the imagination to the delight of young and old alike.

Each selection is a little "gem" reflecting parabolic Bible truths and practical principles of joyful living.

Listed by the Christian Booksellers Association as one of "The Top 10 Bestselling Authors of the Decade," Marjorie Decker is a frequent guest of national radio and television. She is also a recording artist, playwright, and sports enthusiast.

The time-proven value of her Christian Mother Goose® Books to families is a tribute to the Author's lasting contribution to children's literature.

"I'm proud to be the Founder of a Company that distributes books for our future generation. The Christian Mother Goose BIG BOOK is a must for every home with children."

. . . *Earle Fitz*
Founder
RIVERSIDE BOOK & BIBLE HOUSE

"Christian Mother Goose Books have been enthusiastically received by the very young to the 'young at heart.' Scripturally based values are enhanced by inspiring rhyme and prose and charming artwork. Christian Mother Goose Books touch the heart strings, and should be on every family bookshelf."

. . . *Dotty Thur, Owner*
AGAPE BOOKS & GIFTS

"As my children started kindergarten, *I chose* to use Christian Mother Goose for additional reading material to aid them in reading. As they matured to the upper grades, *they chose* to use Christian Mother Goose for poetry and reading projects."

. . . *Karen McMillan*
MOTHER / CALVARY ACADEMY
School Board Officer

"Marjorie Decker's Christian Mother Goose Books are a fun way to point very young children to The Lord. My own two daughters loved them."

. . . Karen Hull
AUTHOR/"THE MOMMY BOOK"

". . . Doing for kiddie devotion what Shakey's did for the pizza."

. . . *Curt Suplee*
THE WASHINGTON POST

"Simple, direct truths, presented in lyrical fashion, wonderfully illustrated with unforgettable characters. I have found the Christian Mother Goose Books to be natural springboards for discussing Christ in my children's world."

. . . *Shelley Gray*
ATTORNEY / MOTHER

"It is a wonderful feeling knowing that God's Words are being shared with our beautiful, young children. Nothing is more capable of spreading those messages than Christian Mother Goose."

. . . *Mickey Rooney*
ACTOR

"Marjorie Ainsborough Decker, through 'Christian Mother Goose,' has taken the negative elements out of nursery rhymes and added a positive, uplifting, scriptural-based meaning. Christian Mother Goose makes nursery rhymes fun and provides children with a higher self esteem."

. . . *Dr. Earl N. VanEaton*
UNIVERSITY DEAN OF EDUCATION

"It is always a special joy to share Christian Mother Goose with our young customers. To see their faces light up as they realize God put Humpty Dumpty together again, just like He will them, makes the business of Christian bookselling all worthwhile."

... *Morris and Samantha Landy*
THE GATHERING PLACE

"Mother Goose, born again and more fun than ever."

... *CHARISMA MAGAZINE*

"The Christian Mother Goose BIG BOOK is planted lovingly in the fields of childhood. These delightful stories and verse are seeds nurtured by God's eternal life. Hidden herein is the genotype of Christ. This sweet book has helped our family and our children grow in their security and love for the Great Gardener.

... *C. Gray Wells III, HORTICULTURIST*
Marcia Wells, MOTHER / TEACHER

"Christian Mother Goose has enriched the young minds that God has placed in our hands. It has blessed not only our children's lives, but ours also."

... *Stephen and Angela Hill*
PARENTS

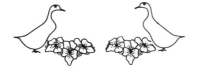

"I have a deep admiration for the beautiful work Marjorie Decker does in sharing The Gospel. Her Christian Mother Goose Audio-Books are loved by the blind around the world, both young and old alike. The blind give thanks for her marvelous books."

... *Ruth Berry Versaw / Director*
LIBRARY FOR THE BLIND

"The rhymes...teach kindness to one another..."

... *John Dart*
LOS ANGELES TIMES

"I have found the Christian Mother Goose Books to be of great value in sharing wholesome Bible Truths with my grand-children. These books are just *delightful!* ...I enjoy them, too. I've often given them as gifts and highly recommend them to families everywhere."

... *Dr. Sibyl Anderson*
OSTEOPATHIC PHYSICIAN /
GRANDMOTHER

"A wise book for caring families!"

... *Marsha Padgett*
NURSE / MOTHER

But these are written that ye might believe that Jesus is the Christ, the Son of God; and that believing ye might have life through His name.

—John 20:31

"...and They All Lived Happily Ever After..."